The Love Challenge

*8 Powerful Keys to Greater Joy,
Spiritual Strength, & Stronger Relationships*

T. D. MURPHY

KAMRYN'S HEART
BOOKS

Copyright ©2015 by Tarrail Murphy

All rights reserved. In accordance with the U.S. Copyright Act of 1976, the scanning, uploading, and electronic sharing of any part of this book without the permission of the publisher is unlawful piracy and theft of the author's intellectual property. If you would like to use material from the book (other than for review purposes), prior written permission must be obtained by contacting the publisher. Thank you for your support of the author's rights.

Kamryn's Heart Books

Unless otherwise noted, all Scripture quotations are taken from THE HOLY BIBLE, NEW INTERNATIONAL VERSION®, NIV® Copyright © 1973, 1978, 1984, 2011 by Biblica, Inc.® Used by permission. All rights reserved worldwide.

Scriptures noted KJV are taken from King James Version.

Italics or bold Scripture quotations have been added by the author for emphasis.

The Love Challenge: 8 Powerful Keys to Greater Joy,
Spiritual Strength, & Stronger Relationships

www.thelovechallenge.us

ISBN: 978-0-6923-9832-6

This book is dedicated to:

My Lord and Savior Jesus Christ
Lord, I thank you for loving me unconditionally.
I thank you for seeing the best of me
even when I was at my worst.

Kamryn
My precious beloved baby girl. Although you're with your
Heavenly Father, your earthly father misses your beautiful smile
sooooo much!

Contents

Introduction	vii
Chapter 1 – The Powerful Key of Patience	1
Chapter 2 – The Powerful Key of Kindness	13
Chapter 3 – The Powerful Key of Biblical Forgiveness	25
Chapter 4 – The Powerful Key of Protecting	39
Chapter 5 – The Powerful Key of Mutual Trust	51
Chapter 6 – The Powerful Key of Hopefulness	63
Chapter 7 – The Powerful Key of Persevering	77
Chapter 8 – The Powerful Key of Unfailing Love	91
Chapter 9 – That's Not Love	113
Chapter 10 – The 21-Day Love Challenge	123
Appendix I – The Love Pledge	129
Appendix II – The Love Prayer	131
Appendix III – The Love Affirmation	133
Appendix IV – The Love Assessment	135
Appendix V – The Love Calendar	137

Introduction

I came to know the eight powerful keys of love during some of the most distressing days of my life. It all began in 2010 while I was on deployment to Afghanistan. Within two weeks of my eight-month deployment coming to an end, I anticipated returning home to be with my family, especially my baby girl, Kamryn, who'd just turned sixteen months old. Leaving her when she was only eight months old to enter a combat zone was one of the hardest things I've ever done. But even that experience could never compare to the one I was about to endure.

One late afternoon, I received a Skype call from Kamryn's mother telling me she was taking Kamryn to the hospital because she was having breathing difficulties. I remember praying for my daughter and hearing within my spirit, "She's good."

Shortly after my prayer, I received a message from my First Sergeant demanding my presence at the Command Post. I quickly grabbed my M-16 service rifle and hurried there, all the while asking myself, "What could he possibly want with me this late?" I walked into his office and saw him holding a telephone. I will never forget the sympathy in his eyes as he handed me the phone. I put the phone to my ear and said, "Hello?"

In a despairing voice, Kamryn's mom told me, "Kamryn died." Suddenly, my whole world turned upside down.

After memorializing her short-lived life, I spiraled into depression, alcoholism, not to mention anxiety from living in eight months of "fight or flight." Thoughts such as, "I only spent half her life with her" and "I should have never left her" played over and over again in my mind, as guilt, pity, anger, and regret taunted me daily.

Some nights, I drove around, slightly intoxicated, looking for her as I said to myself, "Where is she?" "I can't find her." One night when I was driving, I came upon a cliff. Thoughts of allowing my car to fly off the edge flashed across my mind. I had no passion for life. No desire to live. But 1 John 4:8 tells us that God is Love.

Although I wanted to give up on life, Love didn't give up on me. In fact, Love continued to show up through people who loved Him, always bringing me a word of encouragement to see me through. Love was patient with me. Love protected me. Love persevered with me. Love refused to let me go. Each day, Love kept putting His hope in me to accept His love and comfort.

Love didn't give up on me

Even though I nearly gave up on Him, Love didn't hold it against me. Instead, Love kept drawing me to Him through His kindness. When I finally came to Love, He received me with open arms and wrapped them around me. Love gave me rest from my emotional pain. Love strengthened me. Love healed my depression, anxiety, and alcoholism. Love did not fail me. Love was reliable. Love sustained me.

Although a disease called myocarditis took my daughter, she was good, just as the Spirit of Love had assured me that night. She's in the hands of her Creator, pain and trouble free, and it gets no better than that!

I share that part of my life with you to show how powerful the love of God truly is. His powerful love towards me connected my heart to Him. Once our hearts connect to His love, He wants us to connect to the hearts of others out of the love He pours inside of us. John 13:34 says, "A new command I give you: Love one another. **As I have loved you**, so you must love one another." When I think about how loving God has been toward me, even when I have been at my worst, I feel compelled to love others even at their worst.

1 John 4:7 says, "Dear friends, let us love one another, for love comes from God. Everyone who **loves** has been **born of God** and **knows God**." Fulfilling God's command of "Love one another, As I have loved you..." comes by: (1) being born again and (2) knowing God. The word "knowing" can be defined as "experiencing."

Being born again empowers us to follow God's way of loving others. Experiencing God's unconditional love on a personal level, in spite of our flaws, empowers us to continue to love others His way. 1 John 4:19 says, "We love because he first loved us." When we know that He first loved us as sinners, then we can love other sinners, "As He has loved us." God, through Christ, is our model.

Everything has a source and the Source of love is God. 1 John 4:7 reminds us that "love comes from God." As we continue to draw love from Him, we have it to give.

We are like electric circuits and God's love is the electricity flowing within us. A lit bulb of love is evidence of our connection because Jesus calls us the light. Love is evidence that God has turned on that light, a light that shines brighter and brighter as our hearts stay connected to His love.

I feel compelled to say this: never reject within your thinking the fact that God loves you. His loving essence is not based on what you do; it's based on who He is. We cannot change His loving essence; His loving essence changes us. Embrace His love and allow it to embrace you.

Every morning when you get out of bed, know deep within your heart that Jesus loves you. Leave a sticky note on your mirror that says, "My God loves me!" Psalm 92:2 says, "Proclaiming your love in the morning and your faithfulness at night."

Romans 5:5 reminds us that God's love has been poured out into our hearts through the Holy Spirit. Since love is a fruit of the Spirit, it is the Lord who increases it in His people. 1 Thessalonians 3:12 says, **"May the Lord** make your **love increase** and **overflow** for **each other** and for everyone else, just as ours does for you."** Pray often for God to increase His love within your heart and within the hearts of your loved ones.

Praying for our love to increase is important because 1 Corinthians 16:14 says, "Do everything in love." Since God is love, our goal should be to do everything in Him.

If you desire to reconnect and strengthen your relationship in the love of God, you've grabbed the right book. If your desire is to strengthen yourself in God's love, develop spiritual strength, and reclaim your joy, keep reading this book. Whatever your reasons for picking up this book, I believe God will use it not only to strengthen your relationships on a human level, but also to strengthen your relationship with Him.

In just eight chapters, I provide you with eight powerful keys from 1 Corinthians 13:4-8, which I call, "The eight attributes of Biblical love." As you and your loved ones continue to treasure God by loving one another according to His Word, your hearts will be entwined with His and He'll strengthen your relationship. A cord of three strands is not easily broken (see Ecclesiastes 4:12). Neither are hearts entwined with the heart of God.

When you apply the Biblical principles and insights revealed in this book, by building a solid foundation on God's love, you will be able to tear down mental walls of hostility within your relationships. As a result, homes and churches will become stronger in the love of God, making the Body of Christ more effective for our kingdom assignment.

The "That's Not Love" chapter Biblically defines what love is not and what love does not do. Change comes by agreeing with God's definition of unloving actions and attitudes and making an earnest effort to change our unloving ways. The more we empty ourselves of these unloving actions and attitudes, the more room we give God to fill us up with His Spirit of love. As a result, we grow spiritually and become stronger in Him.

I named this book, "The Love Challenge" because loving others God's way challenges our old natures. Glory to God for our new natures, which come from Christ living within our hearts. He provides us with His glorious strength to carry out His will of loving others as He has loved us.

At the end of this book is a 21-Day Love Challenge, which I discuss in greater detail in chapter 10. For three weeks, you and your spouse will pledge to challenge each other to display the eight attributes of Biblical love toward yourself, one another, and anyone else in your lives. Even if you aren't married, take the challenge with your significant other, child, sibling, parent, friend, or even just with yourself. After all, our love for one another is an ongoing debt and our covenant responsibility, whether we're married or single.

The love challenge provides you with Biblical affirmations that will transform your life when you read them with faith. This love challenge allows you and other significant people in your life to work on communicating. During "The Love Assessment" you and your loved one will be able to share your "love needs" in a calm and peaceful manner and invite God into the midst of your relationship through "The Love Prayer." The 21-Day Love

Challenge is a tool to help you and your loved ones grow together in the love of God.

Before we embark on this journey together, however, I must say this: God's love through Christ is the only Perfect Love. It has commanded and empowered us, not to be perfect, but to love out of the perfect love we receive from Him. This is the primary focus of this book.

Chapter 1

The Powerful Key of Patience

Love... is patient.
—1 Corinthians 13:4

A young man had been asking God to send him a wife. In his prayers, he was very specific about the type of woman he wanted God to send him.

One day, he met a beautiful young lady, and they began dating. Soon he discovered God had answered his prayers. She was all he had prayed for and dreamed of. At last, he felt he had found favor with God.

As the months went by, they created a bond and fell deeply in love. Their desire to marry and start a life together grew stronger. He even began looking for an engagement ring.

Although he knew she may have to move across the country because of her job, he was devastated when it actually happened. The young man couldn't understand why God allowed the woman of his prayers to be sent away.

The young man had issues only this experience could solve. He was accustomed to getting what he wanted, when he wanted it, and how he wanted it. And because he always obtained things on his terms, he didn't know how to appreciate them or how to consider others. This time, however, things weren't going to be so easy for him.

If this relationship was going to last and grow into something meaningful, this young man had to mature out of his selfishness and impatience, the underlying causes of his ways. Selfishness and impatience are signs of spiritual immaturity and are toxic to relationships.

If this young man was going to appreciate the love of his life as a wife, and remain committed, he had to develop patience, an important character trait for relationships to flourish. Being apart from the woman of his dreams, as bad as it was for him, helped him do just that.

Patience is the first powerful key needed to increase joy, grow spiritually, and build strong relationships.

Since our most important relationship is with God, we should connect our hearts to His patience. You do so by passing tests He gives you to develop patience in you, and also by accepting how patient He has been with you.

Reflect on God's patience with me for a brief moment. God's patience, revealed through Christ, saved you. His patient hand keeps you from falling. God's patient hand fearfully and wonderfully formed you. Little by little, day by day, He's still patiently forming more of His character in you.

God is patient and diligent in His work. He patiently created the earth in six days when He could have spoken a single word and created it all in an instant. God chose Christ to be a ransom long before the world was formed, but patiently waited to reveal Him in the flesh to free us from sin.

One revelation of how patient God has been with you, will help you become more patient with others, as well as yourself.

That's right; I said *yourself* because in order to love others with the powerful key of patience, you must love yourself by being patient with yourself.

Research shows that being patient with yourself increases your productivity. It removes stress associated with pressure and allows you to increase your thinking capacity. Since God is patient with you, it is all right to be patient with yourself.

> **Be patient with yourself**

The problem is, many people don't understand how patient God truly is. Sadly, they believe falsely that God has a quick temper, a fallacy that Psalm 103:8 exposes: "The LORD is compassionate and gracious, **slow to anger**, abounding in love."

One reason God's anger boils slowly is to give the world time to repent and embrace His love through Christ. 1 Corinthians 13:4-8 teaches us that love is not easily angered.

Falling short does not incite God's anger. We know God takes no pleasure in wrong. His pleasure is in you because you are in His Son, in whom He is well pleased.

At the pool of Bethesda, Jesus healed a man who had been sick for 38 years. John 5:14 says, "Later Jesus found him at the temple and said to him, 'See, you are well again. Stop sinning or something worse may happen to you.'"

Notice how Jesus made him better before requiring him to live a better life. That's what God's patience and grace does—it makes us better, and then requires us to live better lives.

John 12:49 indicates that Jesus only spoke what the Father gave Him to say. Jesus saying, "Stop sinning," therefore, was also the Father saying, "Stop sinning." When Jesus said to the woman caught in adultery in John 8:11, "Neither do I condemn you, 'Go now and leave your life of sin,'" that was the Father speaking through Him. Does this sound like a God who has a quick temper?

Our Father desires the very best for us, never the worst. We must also want the very best for ourselves. Understanding how patient God is and has been toward you, faults and all, will encourage you to take the leaps and bounds necessary to grow in Christ. Because we are in Him, we don't have to walk alone. He left us both His Word and His Spirit to help guide us. We do our part by living according to His Word and not taking His patience for granted.

~The Lord's Helping Hand~

Another way God displays His patience toward us is by helping us. Hebrews 13:6 says, "…The Lord is my helper."

Since our relationship with Christ is like a marriage, in His infinite wisdom God knew it would have done us no good to leave us alone. When Jesus ascended to heaven, therefore, the Father poured out our Helper: the Holy Spirit, who Jesus tells us about in John 14:16: "And I will ask the Father, and he will give you another advocate to **help** you and be with you forever."

The Holy Spirit is ready to help you and me, overcome struggles and grow spiritually. The Psalmists understood this **Kingdom Principle**: Ask and you will receive His help, for Psalm 79:9 says, "**Help us**, God our Savior, for the glory of your name; deliver us and forgive our sins for your name's sake."

While praying for God to help you, pray for God to help your loved ones as well. Our High Priest knows where we are now and He's willing to help us get to where He wants us to be.

He's the Mercy Seat of God, sitting ready to send us help through His Spirit. Hebrews 4:16 says, "Let us then approach God's throne of grace with confidence, so that we may receive mercy and find grace to **help** us in our time of need."

My friend, our Father is on our side. Draw near to Him; He's here to help, for Psalm 54:4 says, "Surely God is my **help**; the Lord is the one who sustains me."

~Let's Be Good Examples~

2 Peter 3:15 declares that God's patience displayed through Christ gives people time to be saved. In His redemptive plan, God desire for us to be examples of His great patience so others might come to know Him. In 1 Timothy 1:16, the Apostle Paul writes:

> "But for that very reason I was shown mercy so that in me, the worst of sinners, Christ Jesus might display his **immense patience** as an example for those who would believe in him and receive eternal life."

The Apostle Paul refused to forget how far God had brought him and the mercy God had shown him. He refused to forget how sinful he was and how patient God was. If God could save him and me, He could save anyone who believes. Lamentations 3:22-23 (KJV) reminds us that, "It is of the LORD's mercies that we are not consumed, because his compassions fail not. They are new every morning: great is thy faithfulness."

Paul's testimony and this Lamentation teaches us the **Kingdom Principle** of never forgetting how merciful and patient God is and has been with us. Let us be good witnesses of His mercy and patience by being merciful and patient with others.

~Developing Great Understanding~

Proverbs 14:29 says, "Whoever is patient has great understanding, but one who is quick-tempered displays folly." This wisdom Scripture is not only speaking a truth, but it is also teaching us this **Kingdom Principle**: We must be patient if we want to become a person of great understanding. Someone who refuses to forget how merciful God has been toward him or her will maintain the type of mindset needed to develop that patience.

This proverb also teaches us that being quick-tempered and being wise are polar opposites. Notice the Scripture says: "…but one who is quick-tempered displays folly."

~Be Patient With God~

Trusting in God helps us become more patient. We can't rush Him anyway. His timing is far better than ours. He knows best and He's always right on time.

A person who submits to God's timing develops the type of patience that leads to great understanding. Being patient with God proves our faith, and faith pleases Him because He's trustworthy. Can you recall a time when He proved to be anything contrary to trustworthy?

According to Galatians 5:22, patience is a fruit of the Spirit. Often, God will produce the fruit of patience in us by giving us a promise and then having us wait for it. Some of you may feel like you've been waiting for the promises of God to come to pass for a very long time. Be encouraged; God has not forgotten His promises to you.

Abraham, the father of faith, waited 25 years to receive what God had promised him. Hebrews 6:15 says, "And so after waiting patiently, Abraham received what was promised."

I urge you to follow Abraham's example of faith. He and Sarah birthed what God had promised because they didn't stop believing. And because they didn't stop believing, they did what they could, and God did what they couldn't.

Don't give up. Keep believing. Stay focused on doing your part while keeping the promises of God near to your heart, for He will deliver. Galatians 6:9 says, "Let us not become weary in doing good, for at the proper time we will reap a harvest if we do not give up."

~Be Patient With Yourself~

Since God is patient with you, my friend, please be patient with yourself. He is doing a great work in you, so let Him complete what He started.

Don't beat yourself up because it actually discourages you. It does nothing to boost your motivation or help you become better. You can maintain a high standard of excellence without being hard on yourself. So relax! A stumble is not failure. Stay strong, get back up, and continue to press on.

Don't compare yourself to others. Be the best you that you can be. Run your own race, at your own pace, without allowing anyone to rush you. Remember, love never rushes; it encourages and motivates.

Being patient with yourself is a genuine form of self-love that will put you at ease and reduce your stress level. It mentally stabilizes you, which improves your overall effectiveness. The more patient you are with yourself, the more patient you will be with others.

~Be Patient With Others~

God never commands us to love in ways He Himself is not willing to love. He's not a hypocrite. **Kingdom Principle**: God will never tell us to do anything He's not willing to do Himself. Rather, He teaches by example, an example that Christ came to earth and set for us to follow.

God will also never ask us to do anything He has not already empowered us to do. Through His Spirit, He has empowered us to live the life He has called us to live. 2 Peter 1:3 says, "His divine power has given us everything we need for a godly life through our knowledge of him who called us by his own glory and goodness."

How is it that a perfect God can be patient with imperfect people? Why can't imperfect people be patient with other imperfect people? God can be patient with us because He knows we are imperfect. Therein lies the key to being patient with others: understanding that we're all imperfect.

The problem lies within our thinking. Jesus is the only perfect person to ever walk the earth. All have sinned and fallen short, except Him. Allowing this Biblical truth to humble us helps us become more patient.

> *The only perfect person to walk the earth was Jesus*

We should never write someone off who's struggling with things we no longer struggle with. "The only time we should look down on another person," the Reverend Jackson said, "is when you are helping them get up."

Jesus said to Peter in Luke 22:32, "...And when you have turned back, strengthen your brothers." God strengthens us so we can strengthen others.

Two people who are patient towards one another unlocks Biblical love. They connect their hearts to the heart of a patient God because they both understand how patient and merciful God has been and still is towards them.

~Never Forget Where You Came From~

A parent who forgets he or she was once a child might be too harsh on his or her immature child. Paul reminds us in 1 Corinthians 13:11 that, "When I was a child, I talked like a child, I thought like a child, I reasoned like a child." Children are supposed to act and think like children. It's a parent's or guardian's responsibility to help them develop sound judgment and good speech. So let's be patient with our children. They are indeed the future. We, the adults, have the responsibility to train them up in God's ways, not tear them down.

By the same token, a church member who forgets how far God has brought him or her might become critically judgmental of other believers who are struggling to overcome. None of us have arrived; rather, we are still arriving. So pray instead of criticizing. Encourage instead of passing judgment. Provide correction and build up. Allow God to work His process. Don't get in the way. Romans 15:7 says, "Accept one another, then, just as Christ accepted you, in order to bring praise to God."

Being patient with one another tears down mental walls of frustration within homes and churches. We are all in the process of recovering from the sin Adam committed in the very beginning. Some of us may be a little further along in our recovery than others, but that doesn't give us the right to judge another. So we must hate the wrong in our lives, confess it, and continue to purge it out of our churches and our homes, but always love one another.

Patience does not mean accepting and tolerating wrong or allowing ourselves to be mistreated. Patience gives us endurance to develop better relationships and encourage our loved ones to live up to their maximum potential. 1 Thessalonians 5:14 says, "And we urge you, brothers and sisters, warn those who are idle and disruptive, encourage the disheartened, help the weak, be **patient with everyone.**"

~Patience And Your Health~

Learning to be patient with God, others, and yourself takes the strain, struggle, and stress off you. Those who are frequently impatient and quick-tempered tend to be overly stressed. We know stress is linked to all sorts of health issues, such as heart disease, stroke, high blood pressure, headaches, etc. God knows what's best for your body. To maintain good health, create strong relationships, and be effective in our kingdom work, we must be patient with others. Ephesians 4:2 says, "Be completely humble and gentle; be patient, bearing with one another in love."

~Key Takeaways~

- God never requires us to put on a characteristic He doesn't wear Himself.
- Patience is a fruit the Holy Spirit produces in us.
- Sometimes God makes us wait. And sometimes we'll find ourselves around others who test that patience. But every time we passed the test, God produces more patience in us. He wants to elevate you, but you must pass the tests.
- If you don't pass a few tests, don't become a dropout. Be patient with yourself. When you round the next corner, you'll be able to take the test again, and this time you'll pass.
- Never forgetting how patient God is with you will help you become more patient.
- The more patient you are with yourself, the more patient you will be with others.
- Remember, there's no such thing as a perfect person or system. There's always room for growth and improvement.
- Raise patient children by setting the example for them to follow.
- Patience is a love key to help us endure with one another as the Holy Spirit conforms us more and more to the image of Christ. He will finally perfect that image when we are glorified with Christ in eternity.
- In the meantime, remember, love is patient.

Chapter 2

The Powerful Key of Kindness

Love is kind.
—1 Corinthians 13:4

A young wife and mother of five had recently dedicated her life to Christ, but grew frustrated with her unsaved husband because he was not fulfilling his role in the household.

Most nights, he would come home late to smell the aroma of a home-cooked meal just to find there was no food left for him because she intentionally only cooked enough for her and the kids.

One night, the Lord pricked her heart by reminding her of how kind He has been toward her, a revelation that not only changed her, but would eventually change her marriage.

She began to avoid quarreling with her husband and no longer left him out of supper. Can you imagine his thoughts when he discovered a plate of food neatly wrapped and waiting for him on the stove? I'm sure he prayed over his meal that night.

Although he recognized her undeserved kindness, months went by with no change. He kept hanging out with his buddies, spending the household money, and coming home late. But instead of saying, "What's the use? He'll never change," she said, "I'll continue to do my part and believe in God to do His."

She replaced complaining with prayer, started washing and folding his clothes, and continued being a loving wife while believing the truth of 1 Peter 3:1, that her husband would come to know Christ through her godly behavior. God was pleased with her actions that proved her faith and He began to change their marriage.

One day, her husband began to wonder what was taking place inside of that church on the corner that was transforming his wife and kids right before his eyes. One Sunday, he decided to go and see for himself.

Eventually, he began attending church with his wife and kids on a regular basis. One day, the Lord answered the young woman's faith and saved him. Afterward, he took his rightful place in the home and began to lead the family in the ways of the Lord.

Because she expressed her faith in love, God drew her husband and anointed him to become a minister of the Gospel and the leader of their church's mission department. That mission provided thousands of winter coats, clothes, pairs of shoes, groceries, hygiene products, and school supplies to thousands of needy kids and families, not only in their local community, but in Belize, Jamaica, Africa, and Haiti, as well. These two have fed thousands of homeless people and led countless souls to Christ.

This is an amazing illustration of how the kindness of Christ working through you can lead souls into the kingdom of God, spread the love of Christ, and transform relationships.

Kindness is the second powerful key needed to increase joy, grow spiritually, and build strong relationships.

~God's Kindness~

Being that our most important relationship is with God, we should connect our hearts to His kindness by accepting how kind He has been towards us. God's kindness, through Christ, saved us. It went out searching for us, found us as lost sinners, and brought us new lives. Romans 2:4 says, "Or do you show contempt for the riches of his kindness, forbearance and patience, not realizing that God's **kindness** is intended to lead you to repentance?" Each day, His kindness allows us to make every effort to do what's right in His sight and we should never take that for granted.

Every day, embrace the fact that God loves you through the abundance of His kindness. Titus 3:4-5 reminds us that God's kindness appeared in Christ to bring salvation to the world, not because we deserve it, but because of His kindness.

~Think About His Kindness~

The Bible teaches us to reflect on God's abundance of kindness. Your perception of God determines your reflection. Who told you God was mean? Who told you His nostrils were flaring against you? God hates sin, but He loves you.

> **Reflect on God's kindness**

Take a few seconds to reflect on God's kindness with me. He never punishes our sins the way He should. In the presence of a holy God, sin is worthy of death, but instead of killing us, He allows us to live.

Because of His grace and mercy, He placed our sins and punishment on the body of an innocent Jesus, who took it and bore it all. It may not be fair, but it is grace. Love covers, love shields, and salvation manifests in the power of God's kindness through Christ.

~Stay In His Kindness~

We must stay connected to God's kindness and never allow negative thinking and unbelief to cut us off from it. Romans 11:22 reminds us to, "**Consider** therefore the kindness and sternness of God: sternness to those who fell, but kindness to you, provided that you **continue in his kindness**. Otherwise, you also will be cut off."

Philippians 4:8 teaches us this **Kingdom Principle**: Think on positive things. Negative things and thoughts may come, but don't allow them to stick. Take captive those negative thoughts and make them subject to Christ. Think on His goodness. The joy of the Lord is your strength.

Never see anything God does as negative. Everything about God is positive. Psalm 145:17 says, "The LORD is righteous in all his ways and faithful in all he does." Even His anger to be released is holy and transmitted to produce right. Positive thinking about God and His loving essence keeps us connected to His joy.

Connect with God's powerful flow of kindness by continually embracing it within your thinking. It will strengthen your bond with Him and increase the fruit of kindness in you. Don't fall away within your thinking. Instead, say to yourself, "My God is good; He is kind toward me."

~Kindness Is Our Witness~

2 Corinthians 6:3-6 reminds us that as servants of God, kindness is one way we witness His kingdom to others. Rude, unkind attitudes and behaviors serve as stumbling blocks to those needing Christ.

The problem is we cannot witness anything we have not seen. Believers who understand that salvation through Christ is a gift of God's kindness become great witnesses of that same kindness to others.

~The Fruit Of Kindness~

Galatians 5:22 teaches us that kindness is a fruit of the Spirit. Jesus reminds us in John 15:5 that apart from Him we can't produce His fruit. Staying connected to His kindness by faith allows the Holy Spirit to produce kindness in us. So continue to draw near to His kindness.

Flaws don't disconnect us from God's kindness. Receiving God's discipline doesn't change the fact that He's still kind. Our actions don't change God's essence. Rather, God's essence produces change in us.

Recognize the times when the Spirit is at work, producing the fruit of kindness in you. Sometimes God will touch your heart to be kind toward someone who has treated you unfairly, or to someone in need, in order to build your character. He wants to elevate you, but you must first pass His character building test.

~Be Kind To One Another~

Ephesians 4:32 says, "Be **kind** and compassionate to one another, forgiving each other, just as in Christ God forgave you." The phrase "one another" in this verse refers to believers. Kindness starts with the house of God before it extends to outsiders. We witness God's kindness to outsiders with integrity by being kind to one another.

> Kindness starts with the church

Unkind speech, actions, and attitudes toward one another elevates mental walls of division that negatively affect the church's mission. God sets the example of kindness by being a kind and forgiving Father. This Scripture teaches us that forgiveness is an act of kindness. Forgiveness knocks down those mental walls of division and reconnect hearts within the church as well as in our homes.

It's not enough to be kind at church. We should be kind in our homes as well. We should produce the fruit of kindness no matter where we are.

~The Male Sets The Example~

A husband sets the tone of kindness within the home. A man of mature love is kind to his wife, children, and pets. Colossians

3:19 says, "Husbands, love your wives and do not be harsh with them." Harshness is to the opposite of love, and kindness is the opposite of harshness. In fact, the Bible tells us that love is kind, and 1 Peter 3:7 teaches that the husband who fails to treat his wife with love hinders his prayers. God also calls wives to respect their husbands. Respect is a form of kindness.

Fathers can discipline their children in a firm, authoritative, and godly manner without being harsh toward them. Both Ephesians 6:4 and Colossians 3:21 indicate that a father's responsibility is to train his children up in the ways of God without disheartening and discouraging them.

Those desiring to be husbands and wives should be practicing kindness toward their significant others. A marriage will consist of whatever attitudes and actions you bring in it. Start developing good habits now.

~Women Have Greater Influence~

While a man may set the example of kindness within the family home, his wife's influence is far greater than his. God created women with a gene I call "great influence." Because of Eve's powerful influence over Adam, he decided to give up his life. Proverbs 14:1 says, "The wise woman builds her house, but with her own hands the foolish one tears hers down." Eve didn't use her influence wisely, and Adam didn't maintain the standard.

A man who maintains godly standards and a woman who uses her influence wisely work well together and build great homes.

~Out With The Old, In With The New~

Removing old habits and replacing them with new ones is how we complement the Holy Spirit's work of producing the fruit of kindness in us.

Ephesians 4:31 reminds us to remove old layers of bitterness, quick tempers, shouting, feelings of ill will, and slandering from our temples, while Colossians 3:12-14 reminds us to put on new layers of kindness and wrap kindness in love. This entire process is accomplished by:

(1) Embracing ourselves as God's chosen people
(2) Embracing ourselves as absolutely loved by God
(3) Embracing one another as imperfect people, and
(4) Embracing forgiveness as we remove one another's guilt, just as God has removed ours.

~Kindness Of Speech~

Every word we speak is a seed. We either plant seeds of life or seeds of death. Planting words of life instead of death into your relationship produces a healthy harvest.

Many relationships are hurting because of negative words and harsh speech. Proverbs 15:1 says, "A gentle answer turns away wrath, but a harsh word stirs up anger."

Harsh speech has the ability to elevate mental walls of resentment, but gentle words knock them down. No one wants to be yelled at, cursed at, or talked at with a sharp and sarcastic tongue. Instead, let's strive to speak to others the way we want them to speak to us. That is the Golden Rule of speech.

If your child acts out, don't say, "You're bad" Or "You're hardheaded." Your words will produce what you plant. Instead say, "You're going to get it right" and "You will obey." Tell them what they did wrong and how to correct their errors. Provide guidance and discipline, and more importantly, pray for your words to land on soft hearts.

~Kindness And Your Health~

Kindness that flows from the heart is said to be beneficial. In fact, research proves kindness has a positive influence on your mental and physical well-being. As you perform kind acts for others, your brain releases chemicals such as oxytocin to provide you with what doctors call the "Helper's High." As a result, you feel good about yourself and what you're doing.

> **Kindness from the heart is good for the heart**

Research suggests that acts of kindness create a sense of interconnectedness, which is what produces the oxytocin in the first place. In turn, the oxytocin, helps you form strong bonds that lead to healthy relationships. 2 Peter 1:7 reminds us that affection must be mutual. Doctors not only agree that unhealthy relationships diminish your health, but also that healthy relationships are just as important to your vitality as regular exercise, sound sleep, and proper diet.

Oxytocin induced by mutual affection will not only benefit your relationship, but it will also benefit your health because it reduces stress and cortisol levels, which in turn may decrease your blood pressure, body aches, headaches, and inflammation.

Oxytocin also neutralizes free radicals and reduces premature aging.

So you see, kindness from you is kind to you.

~Be Kind To Yourself!~

Your body is the dwelling place of God's Spirit. So be kind to it. Respect it. See it as precious and holy. See it as loved by God and set apart for His worship. See it as a house of prayer, an instrument of good works.

Keep your temple clean. Remove all impurities and negative thinking from it. Don't tear your temple down with stress, harshness, criticism, and worry. Don't allow anyone else to tear it down either. Lean on the Chief Cornerstone at all times. Roll every care off you and put it on Him. He's strong enough to handle your cares and mine. God is up 24-7, so be kind to yourself and get some sleep.

Accept that you are forgiven and that you are right in God's sight. Release others from their guilt. Let it go, and forgive yourself.

Allow yourself and others room for error. Be patient. Don't spend too much energy on what's wrong, you need your energy to create solutions and make things right. Learn from mistakes, make emends, and move forward. Keep your conscious clear from guilt and ready for the service of God.

Speak kind words to yourself. Say, "I'm the righteousness of God in Christ," "I can do all things through Christ," or "I'm a beloved child of God."

Researchers agree that people who are kind to themselves are better off mentally and physically than those who mentally beat themselves down. Friends, God is kind toward you. It's all right to be kind to yourself.

~Key Takeaways~

- Embrace within your innermost thoughts how kind God is and has been toward you. We become what we think. You are in Christ by faith and God is pleased with you.
- The Holy Spirit is at work producing kindness in you by leading your heart toward genuine acts of kindness.
- Follow the Spirit's leading and do what's in your heart. All good comes from God.
- Allow God to display His kindness through you so that you can draw lost souls to Him.
- Kindness starts within the house of God. Those in Christ are called to love one another through the bond of kindness.
- Raise children to be kind by setting the example for them to follow.
- Kindness that flows from the heart is good for the heart.
- Acts of kindness in speech and deeds can strengthen you and your relationships.
- Be kind to yourself. Don't tear yourself down with stress and worry. Put it on God. He cares for you.
- Be grateful each day.
- Remember, love is kind.

Chapter 3

The Powerful Key of Biblical Forgiveness

> Love...keeps no record of wrongs.
> —1 Corinthians 13:5

I read a story about a young pilot who became a prisoner of war during World War II. At the prisoner of war camp, he was severely beaten, spat on, starved to the point of malnutrition, and relentlessly tortured each day. Facing death, he said, "God, if you get me out of this alive, I will serve you for the rest of my life."

At the end of the war, he was released back to his military officials and returned home. Although his physical body was free, the memories of his horrific experience were still holding his mind captive.

A war was going on inside his mind as he battled depression and post-traumatic stress. His tormentors visited him each night in the darkness of his nightmares. Every night, he woke up screaming only to discover no one was going to torment him. In order to cope, he turned to alcohol.

Both his life and his marriage were rolling downhill fast. His young wife felt she could no longer bear his alcoholism and bitter rage, until one day she gave her heart to Christ and decided to persevere with her suffering veteran.

In an attempt to honor his wife for not leaving him to his own demise, he decided to accompany her to church. One Sunday, a young preacher gave the invitation, "Receive Jesus as your Savior." The anguished man remembered the promise he had made to God during the war. He kept his word and gave his heart to Jesus. From that day forward, his life was never the same.

The nightmares ceased immediately, and he was healed from depression and alcoholism. His marriage recovered and grew stronger.

He even forgave his captures and tormentors. He eventually returned to their country to meet with some of them. He looked them in the eye and said, "I forgive you."

Using that occasion to give glory to God, he told them about Jesus. At that very moment, some of them accepted Jesus as their Lord and Savior.

As you can see, Biblical forgiveness is a powerful force capable of transforming lives. It has the power to heal mental illnesses, mend broken hearts, restore broken relationships, drive out the spirit of fear, and lead others to Christ.

Biblical forgiveness is the third powerful key needed to increase joy, grow spiritually, and build strong relationships.

~God Sets The Example~

God teaches us how to forgive by forgiving us. Hebrews 8:12 says, "For I will **forgive** their wickedness and will **remember** their sins no more." Remembering our sins no more means that God has released them and does not hold them against us.

The World War II veteran mentioned previously teaches us this **Kingdom Principle**: God forgave him and he's not above God, so his only choice was to forgive others. He would have never experienced God's peace if he'd held his captors and his tormentors guilty in his heart. So he released them of their faults, just as God had released him of his.

~God Dropped The Charges!~

Imagine being on death row waiting to pay the penalty for your wrongs with your life, and one day you receive a pardon letter from the governor that says, "I dropped all the charges against you. By the way, don't feel guilty. Because of your confession, I have made you right in my sight."

I hope you feel as liberated as I do because God the Father has approved our pardon letter, which God the Son has signed with His blood, and God the Holy Spirit has sealed.

Colossians 2:13-14 reads, "When you were dead in your sins and in the uncircumcision of your flesh, God made you alive with Christ. He forgave us **all our sins**, having **canceled the charge** of our legal indebtedness, which stood against us and condemned us; he has **taken it away**, nailing it to the cross."

In other words, God dropped all charges against us more than 2,000 years ago.

~Peace With God~

Since God no longer counts our sins against us because of Christ, we have peace with God. Colossians 1:20 says, "And through him to reconcile to himself all things, whether things on earth or things in heaven, by making peace through his blood, shed on the cross."

Romans 5:1 serves as a second witness of our peace with God: "Therefore, since we have been justified through faith, we have peace with God through our Lord Jesus Christ."

> We are at peace with God

Being assured that God has forgiven you of your sins and has made you at peace with Him because of Christ enables you to forgive and make peace with others. Don't allow Satan, others, or your own negative thoughts to hold your past over your head. When God clears you, you're cleared. Peace starts with faith in Christ as our Prince of Peace, and then becomes a state of being. Be at peace with the fact that God is at peace with you.

Jesus tells us about His peace in John 14:27: "Peace I leave with you; my peace I give you. I do not give to you as the world gives. Do not let your hearts be troubled and do not be afraid."

In this verse, Jesus is teaching us that peace is not determined by external factors. People, money, and situations will never give us internal peace. It only comes by accepting the fact that Jesus spoke it into your heart. You must choose to have it by following the teachings of our Rabbi and not allowing your heart to be troubled. Because the Holy Spirit lives inside you, your peace is found within.

~Forgiveness And Reunion~

Forgiveness restores broken relationships. God, through Christ, restored our relationship with Him. 2 Corinthians 5:19 says, "That God was reconciling the world to himself in Christ, not counting people's sins against them. And he has committed to us the message of reconciliation."

I am just as committed to this message of reconciliation as the apostles were. If God had continued to count our sins against us, we would never have been reconciled with Him. Since we are made in God's likeness, we can ONLY reconcile our relationships by not counting the faults of others against them.

~Biblical Forgiveness~

Biblical forgiveness is forgiving others the way God forgives you. God sets the example for us to follow. Colossians 3:13 reminds us to "Bear with each other and forgive one another if any of you has a grievance against someone. **Forgive as the Lord forgave you.**"

Biblical forgiveness means we forgive all sins committed against us, settle all accounts, and cancel all charges. In doing so, we no longer see others as guilty but declare them right in our sight.

Matthew 6:14 reminds us, "For if you forgive other people when they sin against you, your heavenly Father will also forgive you."

~As The Lord Forgave You!~

Notice the previous Scripture says, "Forgive as the Lord forgave you." How did the Lord forgive you? By clearing your guilt, keeping it in the past, and making you right in His sight. Knowing exactly how the Lord forgave us teaches us how to properly forgive others.

> *Forgive as the Lord forgave you*

Psalm 103:12 says, "As far as the east is from the west, so far has he removed our transgressions from us." To forgive as the Lord forgives us comes by removing the transgressions of others far from our hearts.

~Releasing~

Research proves that negative events leave deeper marks on the brain than positive ones. Releasing the past may be difficult for most because feelings of hurt, distrust, bitterness, and disappointment are all birthed by negative events. Releasing negative events, however, is the key to releasing all the negative emotions associated with them, freeing yourself, and moving forward.

Relationships, whether we're talking about husband and wife, parent and child, church partners, or friends who hang onto the past cannot progress. Releasing the past does not change it, but it certainly makes room for the future. It's hard to focus on the present and future while carrying around the dead weight of the past. The only thing we can do about the past is let it go.

Releasing the past does not mean we will forget it. On the contrary, our minds are like computers with large amounts of memory, and there's no software we can use to permanently delete it. Unlike computers, we also think and feel. For these reasons, we must decide to let go of the past and give it to God. Romans 8:28 says, "And we know that in all things God works for the good of those who love him, who have been called according to his purpose." All things include past hurts and past disappointments.

> The only thing we can do about the past is leave it behind

~Forgiveness, Mercy, And Prayer~

In Mark 11:25, Jesus says, "And when you stand **praying**, if you **hold anything against anyone**, forgive them, so that your Father in heaven may forgive you your sins." The Lord teaches us this **Kingdom Principle**: In order to receive God's forgiveness, we must forgive others by not holding anything against them. This is also true when coming before God in prayer.

Prayer and forgiveness go together because every time we pray, we appear before God's Mercy Seat where we receive His continual flow of mercy and forgiveness. In the Old Testament, after the high priest covered the Mercy Seat with the blood of animals, Israel was able to receive mercy from God. Without the blood, however, there could be no mercy.

One of the reasons Jesus sits at the right hand of the Father is because He is the Mercy Seat. We pray in Jesus' Name because His covering gives us the ability to communicate with God. Every time we come before God in prayer, we appear before His Mercy.

> *Always appear before a merciful God having mercy for others inside of your heart*

If we come before God while holding something against someone in our hearts, however, we are failing to recognize the Mercy He extends to us through Christ.

The Lord teaches us to pray with a spirit of mercy: "Forgive us our debts, as we also have forgiven our debtors." Jesus teaches us this **Kingdom Principle**: Before asking for God's release, we must first release others. We should all ponder the question, "Who am I to appear before a merciful God and ask for His mercy to change my situation if I have no mercy inside my heart?" In Luke 6:36 Jesus says, "Be merciful, just as your Father is merciful."

Jesus leaves us with this declaration in Matthew 5:7: "Blessed are the merciful, for they will be shown mercy."

~Stop Bringing It Up!~

According to Revelation 12:10, Satan brings up our offenses before God day and night because He wants to separate us from God's love. Out of God's love for us, however, Christ shuts him down and covers the matter.

Love covers. Since God's love through Christ covers us, He expects us to cover others. Proverbs 17:9 says, "Whoever would foster love **covers** over an offense, but whoever **repeats** the matter separates close friends."

Covering an offense means to stop bringing it up. If we continue to bring up someone's offense, we drag that person and ourselves back into the past, creating a mental wall of division.

If Proverbs 17:9 teaches us that love covers and repeating an offense separates, then bringing up the past is unloving (this is what Satan does) and leaving the past behind keeps our relationships together (this is what Christ does). Let us choose to be like Christ.

~Peace Together~

We are called to be peacemakers. Hebrews 12:14 reminds us to make an earnest effort to live in peace with everyone, including those we are in relationship with.

I feel compelled to say this, however: living in peace with someone may require living apart. Peace may come by leaving an unfaithful partner or leaving an abusive relationship. Love doesn't force anyone to be faithful, and no one has to live in abuse.

A peaceful relationship environment comes when two people desire to live in harmony with the Spirit of God. This takes effort. Ephesians 4:3 says, "Make every effort to keep the unity of the Spirit through the bond of peace."

~Relationships Over Offerings~

In His Sermon on The Mount, Jesus preached that God honor relationships more than He honors offerings. Matthew 5:23-24 says, "Therefore, if you are offering your gift at the altar and there remember that your brother or sister has something against you, leave your gift there in front of the altar. First go and be reconciled to them; then come and offer your gift."

Refusing to follow the Lord's teaching makes our offerings no good with Him. He's a God of order. As His disciples, we are responsible for making an earnest effort to restore a relationship. If the other person refuses your hand of reconciliation, however, don't hold it against him or her. Don't become bitter. Pray for them. The Lord will honor you as well as your offering for honoring His Word.

~Forgive Yourself~

God, the Ultimate Authority, does not hold your record of wrong against you, so why hold it against yourself? Practice genuine self-love by forgiving yourself.

> *God forgave you so forgive yourself*

Don't live in mental condemnation. Condemnation kills. Many believers are killing themselves with stress because they feel guilty for past mistakes. But since there's nothing you can do to change them, leave them in the past.

2 Corinthians 7:10 says, "Godly sorrow brings repentance that leads to salvation and leaves no regret, but worldly sorrow

brings death." Peter's and Judas' responses to their sins against Jesus show us what godly and worldly sorrow look like.

Both men acknowledged their sin internally, though Judas acknowledged his aloud, as well. But even though both men were sorry, Peter humbled himself under God's grace and lived to become a great Apostle. Judas did not. Judas hanged himself under the letter of the law and received eternal death.

These two examples teach us some key things about sin, grace, and the law. The Spirit of grace says, "You've messed up, but I'm going to let you live, and by the way, you're going to do some great things for God's kingdom. You've stumbled, but I'm going to keep you from falling. Turn around and follow Me." The letter of the law, on the other hand, says, "You've messed up and you're worthy of death. Kill yourself emotionally and spiritually." Condemnation says, "You're a failure."

> Grace says, "I've come to give you life"

Jesus did not come to take life out of you. He came to deposit life into you and give you more of it. He came to give you joy. Receive it! Accept the grace God has freely given you; it will transform your life. God wants us living under His grace; it strengthens us and empowers us to do great things for Him and others.

~Are You Living Under Law Or Grace?~

Those living under the law believe what they do makes them right with God. They are usually very prideful people who are critical and judgmental of others. When they do good they feel as if they're standing on their own rock and when they do bad, they feel condemned as if they've fallen out of God's good graces.

God is the only lawgiver and judge. He did not create the law for us to see if we are right with Him or not or for us to judge and condemn others or ourselves. He created the law to teach us right from wrong. Romans 3:20 says, "Therefore **no one** will be declared righteous in God's sight by the works of the law; rather, through the law we become conscious of our sin."

We wouldn't know what sins such as envy, lying, adultery, or gossip were if we didn't have the law telling us what they were. If you do sin, don't focus on the law. Be like Peter and focus on grace, repentance, and Christ's restoration.

God made you right in His sight when you placed your faith in Jesus. Romans 3:28 says, "I mean we are made right with God through faith, not through what we have done to follow the law. This is what we believe."

Now that God has made us right, He wants our obedience from the heart. He wants us to walk upright before Him. It's important to remember, however, that our obedience will never exceed the righteousness of the blood of Christ. Obedience should come from a place of belief that says, "My faith in Christ makes me right. Because I love Him, I want to live right." Galatians 3:11 reminds us that, "Clearly no one who relies on the law is justified before God, because "the righteous will live by faith."

Faith in Christ alone makes us righteous. And out of that faith, we make every effort to prove our faith by living righteously. Abraham, the father of faith, believed in God first, and his obedience proved his faith. Romans 4:3 reads, "What does Scripture say? "Abraham believed God, and it was credited to him as righteousness."

~Receiving God's Grace~

God always extends His grace to us before requiring us to live better lives. Here's a **Kingdom Principle**: Receiving God's abundance of grace is the key to becoming all that God has created you to be in Christ.

Judas did not receive God's abundance of grace and it killed him. Peter did, and he received abundant life. A person living under grace does not take God's grace for granted. Those living under God's grace understand that it empowers them to carry out His will. Embracing God's grace within our hearts and minds empowers us to grow in God. 2 Peter 3:18 says, "But grow in the grace and knowledge of our Lord and Savior Jesus Christ. To him be glory both now and forever! Amen."

~Don't Put It Off~

Benjamin Franklin once said, "Don't put off until tomorrow what you can do today." Proverbs 27:1 teaches us that we do not know what tomorrow may bring. Today is the day, my friend, to call someone and say, "I'm sorry." Today is the day to forgive.

~Key Takeaways~

- Biblical forgiveness comes from a pure heart. It comes from a heart that understands you are truly forgiven by God.
- It comes from a heart that understands you are completely reconciled with God because of Christ.

- Biblical forgiveness comes from a heart that says, "I dare not come before God's Throne of Mercy in prayer if I have no mercy in my heart for others."
- Releasing the faults of others can reconcile relationships.
- Declaring others "not guilty" tears down any mental walls of hostility that separates you from them.
- Since God no longer holds your past against you, don't hold your past against yourself. When you confess sin, God releases; therefore, release yourself and move toward your purpose.
- Accepting that you are forgiven by God empowers you to forgive yourself and others, which allows you to move forward in God's great love and purpose.
- Remember, love forgives, it releases, and it covers.

Chapter 4

The Powerful Key of Protecting

Love…always protects.
—1 Corinthians 13:7

One summer night, a man picked up his wife and one of her co-workers after a meeting they had at work. He and his wife were going to drop off the co-worker and then head home.

When they arrived at the co-worker's apartment, the man got out of the car and walked her to the lobby, while his wife remained in the car. Since they lived on the Southside of Chicago, she locked all the doors, though he left the keys in the ignition.

He made sure the co-worker made it inside her apartment safely and walked back to his car. As he approached the door, a man ran up to him with a gun. "Give me your money," he demanded, as he pushed the gun against the man's stomach. After the man showed him an empty wallet, the robber then demanded he hand over his car keys.

"They are in the car," he said.

The robber looked inside the car and saw the man's wife. "Tell her to open the door," he insisted.

He refused in order to protect his wife. The robber then poked him in the stomach with his gun and said, "Do it, or I'll kill you." He refused again. The robber became even more frustrated and his tone of voice grew even more angry as he continued making his demands.

Even though his wife couldn't hear the conversation from inside the car, she could clearly see her husband being held up at gunpoint. I could only imagine her train of thought as she witnessed this horrifying scene. Calling the cops wasn't an option because she didn't have a cell phone. She could have gotten out of the car, blown her horn and caused a distraction, or driven away and left her husband, but she decided to pray and wait.

A city bus stopped just shy of the vehicle. The activity surrounding the bus somewhat distracted the robber and he momentarily pulled the gun away from the man's stomach. At that moment, the man saw an opportunity to make a quick move. Since he was much taller and heavier than the robber, he felt he could take him and cease the gun. Not willing to take the chance that something would go wrong, however, he decided just to remain calm.

As the bus drove off, he placed his hand on the young robber's shoulder and said, "Look here; this isn't right. What you're doing just isn't right. The next car might be a policeman, and you could get killed or sent to jail for this."

The robber placed the gun back in the man's stomach, continued his demands, and threatened to kill him once again. When he refused again, the robber hesitated for a moment, stuck the gun in his pocket, and ran away.

The man's wife hurriedly unlocked the door and she and her husband drove off, thanking God.

This brings me to the fourth powerful key that increases joy, grows spiritually, and builds strong relationships: protecting.

~Protected By God's Power~

Friends, we are protected and shielded by the power of God. No protection is better than that!

We are protected by the same power that said, "Let there be light!" The same power that not only created the universe, but also sustains it.

We are protected by the same power that aligns the moon perfectly with the sun to illuminate it, the same power that opens the heavens and releases rain upon the face of the earth, the same power that raised Christ from the dead, and the same power that brought us into His salvation.

~Embrace His Protection~

Embrace God's protection within your thinking. You are His most prized possession. He bought you with the precious blood of Jesus and anointed you with His Spirit as an assurance of your salvation. God has an invested interest in you. He protects His investment. He protects what He loves.

Taking refuge in God's power of protection is an act of faith that pleases Him. It shows God that we trust Him. The Psalmist David fully embraced God's protection in Psalm 32:7 when he said, "You are my hiding place; you will protect me from trouble and surround me with songs of deliverance."

~Protected Salvation~

God's love and protection removes all fear. So if we embrace them, we won't live in fear. Matthew 10:28 reminds us not to fear anyone but God. Even though we should never be afraid to come to Him because He's our Father, we should be afraid to live life without Him.

No one can take eternal life from us. God Himself protects our salvation. Jude prays in 1:24, "To him who is able to keep you from stumbling and to present you before his glorious presence without fault and with great joy—to the only God our Savior be glory, majesty, power and authority, through Jesus Christ our Lord, before all ages, now and forevermore! Amen." It is God who keeps us standing. Our part is to stand firm in Him. 1 Corinthians 16:13 says, "Be on your guard; stand firm in the faith; be courageous; be strong."

Satan wishes to kill, steal, and destroy our faith. In John 17:15 Jesus intercedes for us saying, "My prayer is not that you take them out of the world but that you protect them from the evil one."

In John 10:28 Jesus says, "I give them eternal life, and they shall never perish; no one will snatch them out of my hand." When someone tries to snatch something out of your hand, like a purse or a piece of paper, he or she uses great force. The hand of the Lord is so strong and mighty that an attempted snatch won't faze Him. Anyone Jesus places His hand on belongs to

Him, period. Our eternal life is secured in Him.

> **We're secured by the Lord's mighty hand**

His mighty hand keeps the enemy at bay. Exodus 15:6 says, "Your right hand, LORD, was majestic in power. Your right hand, LORD, shattered the enemy." It is His hand that strengthens, protects, and keeps us from falling. Like a little kid, we must hold on to it.

~Protecting Others~

You protect what you love. Although God is the ultimate protector, He has called us to love others through His Spirit of protection. After all, it was that Spirit who protected the gentleman and his wife I mentioned previously.

> **You protect what you love**

We are not only called to protect our loved ones from outsiders, but we are also called to protect our loved ones from ourselves, a point often overlooked within relationships. No one wants to see the person he or she loves hurting.

~Love Doesn't Hurt~

Romans 13:10 says, "Love does no harm to a neighbor. Therefore love is the fulfillment of the law." We must decide not to intentionally hurt the ones we love, physically or emotionally. That is how we protect one another.

I must say this, however: hurting another's feelings or offending someone, however slight, doesn't mean there's no love. It only is a clear indicator that some adjustments need to be made. One of our goals as believers is to operate in a love that seeks not to harm another. God's Spirit has empowered us to achieve this goal.

~Ouch! It Hurts~

Galatians 5:15 says, "If you bite and devour each other, watch out or you will be destroyed by each other." The Apostle Paul teaches us that harmful actions toward one another is destructive.

Most people don't realize how much pain they bring upon others because of their words or misdeeds. Paul tells us to "watch out," as if he wants us to wake up and be aware of how hurtful behavior can and will destroy any relationship.

Such awareness is the beginning of change. In Galatians 5:16, Paul teaches us what we need to do to make a real and lasting change in our behavior so that we will not hurt the ones we love: "So I say, walk by the Spirit, and you will not gratify the desires of the flesh." Gratify means to satisfy. Scholars define the word "flesh" as the old sinful nature.

The desires of the sinful nature, which will always be ungodly, are often satisfied by disregarding the feelings of others. The sinful nature doesn't care who it hurts in order to satisfy its desires and will seek that satisfaction by any means necessary.

~Walk By God's Spirit~

God provides the solution to this problem in Galatians 5:16 – to walk in the Spirit. By doing so, God promises us that we WILL NOT gratify the desires of the sinful nature. God's Word is true, and He willed for us not to gratify sinful desires. So we must be willing to do our part and walk by the Spirit. How is this accomplished?

~How Do I Walk By The Spirit?~

Walking by the Spirit began when we were born again. Jesus says in John 6:37, "All those the Father gives me **will come** to me, and whoever comes to me I will never drive away." When you heard the Father tugging on your heart to dedicate your life to Jesus, the Spirit was leading you to come.

Jesus further declares in John 6:44, "No one can come to me unless the Father who sent me **draws them**, and I will raise them up at the last day." The sovereign God drew your heart toward Jesus. The moment you came to Him, you were walking by the Spirit.

That same tug that prompted your heart to dedicate your life to Christ is the same tug that prompts your heart to follow the Spirit. Stay in tuned with that tug because that is God speaking to you through the Holy Spirit. Romans 8:14 says, "For those who are led by the Spirit of God are the children of God."

Galatians 3:3 teaches us that we began our spiritual journey through the Holy Spirit. Galatians 3:3 reads, "Are you so foolish? After **beginning** by means of the Spirit, are you now trying to finish by means of the flesh?" The Apostle Paul teaches us that trying to finish our spiritual journey in the flesh—in our own might—is foolish. We must continue to walk by faith in God's Word.

Galatians 5:25 says, "Since we live by the Spirit, let us keep in step with the Spirit." We received new birth by the Spirit of God, and God is the one who called us to continue to live by His Spirit. Our spiritual journey, therefore, is a daily faith walk with God.

When we obey God's Word, we are walking and keeping in step with the Spirit. God promises us that if we follow the Spirit's leading: the spoken and written Word of God, we **will not** fulfill the desires of the sinful nature. As a result, we will protect ourselves and others from the old nature's harmful ways.

~Evidences Of Walking By The Spirit~

Not satisfying the desires of the sinful nature is one of the evidences that we are walking by the Spirit. The sinful nature wars against the Holy Spirit, who directs our hearts into the will and Word of God. Romans 8:13 reminds us that we kill the misdeeds of the flesh by the Spirit. Ephesians 6:17 teaches us that the Sword of the Spirit is the Word of God. The more we read, hear, and obey God's Word, the Sword of the Spirit, the better we become at killing off the misdeeds of our sinful nature.

Evidence of the fruit of the Spirit in our lives is another proof that we are walking by the Spirit. Galatians 5:22-23 identifies these fruits as love, joy, peace, forbearance, kindness, goodness, faithfulness, gentleness, and self-control. We should see the fruit of God's Spirit popping out in our daily actions.

~Avoid The Argument~

One of the main reasons many relationships are filled with so much disharmony is because of constant arguing. Galatians 5:19-20 teaches us that discord is evidence that we are walking in the old sinful nature. Peace, on the other hand, is evidence that we are walking by the Spirit. God called us to be peacemakers, not troublemakers. During the Sermon on the Mount, Jesus said, "Blessed are the peacemakers, for they will be called children of God."

Proverbs 20:3 says, "It is to one's honor to avoid strife, but every fool is quick to quarrel." This wisdom Scripture teaches us that God wants us to avoid arguments for our own good. Those who argue usually do so in circles trying to prove their points, all the while getting nowhere.

Arguing puts us in "fight or flight" mode where we tend to perceive everything someone else says as a threat. This is why we act defensively when arguing. As a result, our tone of voice hardens. We may not hear this change in our tone, but we certainly hear the other person's tone. We become more alert—not to listen—but to argue.

As a result, rational thinking diminishes and we may end up saying things we shouldn't have said. In the end, the only things that get accomplished are elevated blood pressure, wasted energy and time, and unhealthy stress. These are reasons Proverbs 20:3 teaches us that arguing is foolish.

The Love Challenge

We must protect our relationships with one another and each other's health by avoiding arguments. Calm down. Take a walk. Come back when you're more at peace and express how you feel in a calm manner. Submit to one another by respecting one another's viewpoints. Place them in God's hand of justice and allow Him to be the judge. It takes two to argue, but it only takes one wise person to avoid an argument. Philippians 2:14 says, "Do everything without grumbling or arguing."

~Protecting Yourself~

Protecting ourselves from the destructive behaviors of the sinful nature is key to genuine self-love. If we don't honor and protect our own physical, mental, and spiritual health, it's going to be impossible to operate in the type of protective love God desire us to have toward others.

Good decision making is one way we protect our lives and guard our soul salvation. Proverbs 2:11 says, "Discretion will protect you, and understanding will guard you." Our discretion, understanding, and judgment should be guided by the Word of God because we know His Word is true.

Protect yourself with good judgment

Sound judgment comes from wisdom, and wisdom comes from God. If we lack wisdom, James 1:5 tells us to ask for it and He will give it. Our heavenly Father stands willing and ready to impart wisdom to all His children who ask confidently.

Another way we protect ourselves is by cultivating a spirit of thanksgiving. 1 Thessalonians 5:18 reminds us to "Give thanks in all circumstances; for this is God's will for you in Christ

Jesus." Thanksgiving keeps us humble and protects us from pride. It helps us understand that all good come from God, including our talents, skills, abilities, and possessions.

Thanksgiving also protects us from negative emotions such as self-pity, envy, and the ideas that we don't have anything to be grateful for or that we're "missing out." Thanksgiving helps us become content and pleased about what God has done and what He's doing now. It also unlocks what God is going to do for you in the future.

Researchers agree that daily gratitude makes us happier, reduces stress, and increases social intellect and focus. These changes take place through a process called neuroplasticity.

Neuroplasticity is a term used to describe the rewiring of our brains to form and strengthen new brain connections: thoughts, behaviors, and feelings, while weakening the old ones. The more we use these new pathways and the less we use the old ones, the more older ones eventually fade away. Romans 12:2 reminds us to be transformed by the renewing of our minds. That scripture was written more than 1,900 years ago, and neuroscientist has just caught up.

By repeatedly embracing negative responses to given stimuli, the pathway of negative emotions such as bitterness, rage, envy, and stress becomes stronger. It's similar to lifting weights. The more we lift, the stronger we become. The more negative thoughts we lift, the stronger negative responses becomes.

Instead of lifting up pride, self-pity, anger, isolation, disappointment, and other negative emotions, lift up thanksgiving to God and become stronger in Him. Repeatedly responding to negative situations with thanksgiving allows the brain to create a new pathway that will strengthen and become habitual over time.

The power behind neuroplasticity and creating new pathways that renew the mind is repetition. This is why God tells us to give thanks in all circumstances.

Protect your mental health with gratitude If you find yourself in pain, say, "God, I thank you." If you find yourself feeling good say, "Lord, thank you." Watch God change your life when you express your gratitude to Him in all occasions, good or bad.

~Key Takeaways~

- God protects those He loves.
- We have eternal protection sealed by the Holy Spirit. No one can take that away.
- Rest and remain in God's protection.
- Protect the Name of God by living holy. That is how we display our love and respect for Him.
- Those who protect God's Name understand they represent His kingdom wherever they go—on the job, at home, at church, or any other public place.
- Loving others with the bond of protection means not intentionally allowing our speech or actions to hurt them in any way.
- If we do offend or hurt another, we protect the relationship from further damage by doing our best to make amends and reconcile with them. We prove our love for others by not repeating the same actions that caused the pain.
- Protecting ourselves from negative thinking, sin, and dangerous actions is the true definition of self-love.
- Friends, love protects.

Chapter 5

The Powerful Key of Mutual Trust

Love...always trusts.
—1 Corinthians 13:7

A young man received a vision from God to move his family from Texas to Southern California to start a church. The problem was they had no money, no members, no buildings, and no sponsors. In fact, this young couple did not have a single friend in the city. Furthermore, the young man had no experience whatsoever as a senior pastor.

The young man communicated his vision to his wife: "Honey, I think God wants us to move to Southern California and start a church, "What do you think?"

This would mean leaving a familiar land and embarking on an unknown journey in an unknown territory with unknown results. Knowing all of this, the young lady said to her husband, "It scares me to death. But I believe in God, and I believe in you, so let's go for it."

If this couple had not trusted in God and in their relationship, church history as we know it would be much different today, for God would have not used them to open Saddleback Church in Lake Forest, California. There would not be nine locations nationally, to date, nor would there be four international locations in Germany, Argentina, Hong Kong, and the Philippines.

God would have not used them to baptize more than 20,000 people over the last 10 years. There would be no Purpose Driven Life or Peace Plan, both of which God continues to use to transform lives. God would not have used this family to train and equip more than a half million pastors in more than 160 countries.

The lives of Pastor Rick Warren and his wife, Kay, would be totally different if there had been no trust. God's trust in them, their mutual trust in God, and their trust for one another, was essential in God's plan for their lives.

The faith step they took more than 33 years ago proved their mutual trust. It cast out all fear and God is getting the increase. Countless lives continue to be saved and transformed daily. This is what the power of trust in God and one another have the ability to do.

Mutual trust is the fifth powerful key needed to increase joy, grow spiritually, and build strong relationships.

~Does God Trust Us?~

Jesus cultivated strong relationships with His disciples by trusting them and earning their trust. Even when Thomas doubted Jesus' resurrection, He appeared to him and erased the doubt from his mind. If Jesus and His disciples were to operate in love and accomplish God's will, He had to trust them and they had to trust Him.

God, through Christ, trusts us with the Great Commission, which is, "Go ye therefore and teach all nations." And to carry out this commission, He entrusted us with His Spirit.

God also trusts us with the spiritual gifts He gives us to be used for His glory and for the building of His church. He also trusts us with the keys to His kingdom, and has given us the authority to get things moving, both in heaven and on earth through prayer. God entrusted us with talents, skills, and abilities. He has an expectation that we prove trustworthy by producing good works.

~Prove Trustworthy~

Because God has trusted us with His anointing, authority, and gifts, He wants us to prove ourselves trustworthy. Jesus tells us in Luke 16:10, "Whoever can be **trusted** with very little can also be trusted with much, and whoever is dishonest with very little will also be dishonest with much."

The more trustworthiness we prove with little, the more we can be trusted with much. Those who desire God to bless them with a marriage, for example, should first prove their trustworthiness in the dating relationship. Those who desire God to increase their income should first prove their trustworthiness with their current income. Pastors who desire God to grow their churches should first prove their trustworthiness with their tiny congregations.

> *We must prove trustworthy*

~Mutual Trust~

In order for any relationship to operate in love, including our relationship with God, there must be mutual trust. God places His trust in us and we must place our trust in Him. God will never force anyone to trust Him. He proves His trustworthiness and then exhorts us to trust Him for our own good.

~Trust And Treasure God Above All~

A relationship without trust is risky and shaky. We don't need to feel that way in our relationship with God. After all, when was the last time He failed? Never. When was the last time He lied? He's not a man to lie. God is worthy of our trust.

God's Word is as high as His Name, which is only as good as His Word. And we know God's Word is trustworthy. Luke 1:37 says, "For **no word** from God will ever fail."

Those who trust in God are not afraid to draw near to Him. They always come to God in their time of need. Instead of running away from God because of struggles, they draw near to Him for grace and mercy to help them overcome.

The Bible teaches us to never trust in anything or anyone more than our God. Our trust must be in God first and foremost because He's the only constant in a changing and uncertain world. A job is not the primary source of provision; God is. Relationships may bring happiness; but God is our Source of ultimate joy. Beauty may fade; God lasts forever.

We will never go wrong by trusting and treasuring God above all. Jesus says in Matthew 6:21, "For where your treasure is, there your heart will be also." Nothing or no one can destroy a heart that is with God.

Trust and treasure God above all

~The Names Of God~

Throughout the Old Testament, God reveals Himself to us through His Names. The Names of God allow us to grasp a better understanding of who God is, teach us the many ways God desires us to trust in Him, and help us discover the many ways He cares for us.

- Jehovah-Jireh means, "The Lord will provide" (see Genesis 22:14). We can trust in God to provide for our every need.
- Jehovah-Nissi means, "The Lord is my Banner" (see Exodus 17:15). God is our rallying point of victory. We can trust in Him to fight battles that are too big for us.
- Jehovah-Shalom means, "The Lord is Peace" (see Judges 6:24). We can trust in God to give us peace in any and every situation.
- Jehovah-Maccaddeshcem means, "The Lord your Sanctifier" (see Exodus 31:13). The Lord sanctifies and sets us apart for His purpose. We can trust in Him to continue to cleanse us and present us flawless unto Himself.
- Jehovah-Rohi means, "The Lord my Shepherd" (see Psalm 23:1). We can trust in our Good Shepherd to care for, lead, protect, and guide us just as a shepherd cares for his sheep.

The Love Challenge

- Jehovah-Tsidkenu means, "The Lord our Righteousness" (see Jeremiah 23:6). We can trust that we are righteous because the Lord makes us righteous by His blood and by His Holy Spirit.
- Jehovah-Rapha means, "The Lord who heals" (see Exodus 15:26). We can trust in the Lord to heal our broken hearts and illnesses, now and in eternity.
- Jehovah-Shammah means, "The Lord is there" (see Ezekiel 48:35). We can trust that the Lord is always with us.

~Trust In His Direction~

The more we trust in God, the more He reveals to us. Trust in God allows Him to direct our steps toward accomplishing many great things. We may not fully understand why God is directing our steps the way He is, but our part is to trust in the Word He has placed in our hearts and continue to march.

During the Battle of Jericho, God ordered Joshua to march the army of Israel around the city once a day for six days and to instruct seven priests to carry trumpets made out of rams' horns in front of the ark. On the seventh day, God ordered them to march around the city seven times, with the priests blowing the trumpets. On the final lap, the priests were to give a long blast, and the whole army was to give a loud shout and attack as soon as the wall collapsed. God ordered their steps, but they had to do the walking.

Joshua didn't have to understand these steps because He knew God's voice. Jesus says in John 10:27, "My sheep listen to my voice; I know them, and they follow me." Joshua trusted in

God. He followed the steps God ordered him to take, and God gave him success.

God's ways are not our ways. His ways are far better. Joshua and his men would have not been able to knock the wall down using their own abilities. God placed His super on their natural because they proved they trusted Him by taking the steps He ordered them to take. As long as we trust the Who, we don't have to fully understand the what, when, where, how, and why. Just focus on doing what God requires of you today.

Take the first step. He put the strategy in your heart for a reason. Get moving! There are great things on the other side of that wall. It has been blocking you for too long. It's time for it to come down. Your business is on the other side of that wall. Your very first CD production is on the other side of that wall. Your college degree is on the other side of that wall. Take the steps and be diligent. Commit your work to God. Always ask Him to strengthen your hands and He will.

~Trust God With Your Life~

Why not trust God with the very life He has given you? After entering into His kingdom, God never wants us to put our trust in the world's system again. By faith, we release Him to be involved in all things pertaining to us, including money, relationships, decisions, emotions, thoughts, plans, protection, salvation, and provision. And when we do so, He blesses us. Jeremiah 17:7 says, "But blessed is the one who trusts in the Lord, whose confidence is in him."

> **God blesses those who trust in Him**

~No Where Else To Turn~

Sometimes God allows us to get into situations where we have no other alternative but to trust in Him. Some of you reading this chapter may be at that place right now. Here's a **Kingdom Principle**: When you feel you have no other choice but to trust God, He is preparing to elevate you. He wants to take you to new heights in your relationship with Him. Your trust in Him, and not giving up, is about to take you there.

Jesus, stretched out and nailed to the cross, had nowhere else to turn but to God the Father. Although He could have, He didn't remove Himself from the cross. Instead He turned to the Father in a loud voice and said, "Father, into your hands I commit my Spirit."

We must be like our Lord and say, "Father, into your hands I commit my life. I commit my finances. I commit my relationships. I commit my desires." We must say, "God I transfer, entrust, and dedicate all things to you." "God, I trust you."

~Trust, Mental Stability, & Peace~

People, thoughts, and situations will always try to make you doubt God. This is why we must trust in Him with all our hearts, so He can move us into His peace and give us mental stability to move toward His promises. Isaiah 26:3 says, "You will keep in perfect peace those whose **minds are steadfast**, because they **trust in you.**"

The more we trust in God, the more stable we become. Trust in God lowers our stress. It realigns chemical imbalances and brings us into His peace. He created us; therefore, He knows exactly what we need to live healthy and peaceful lives.

~Cultivating Trusting Relationships~

God created us to be relational beings. It is His will for us to cultivate trusting relationships. A relationship that operates in trust grows to become a powerful one. Trust must be mutual, however, in order for the relationship to operate in love. All parties must, therefore, prove trustworthy.

The key to cultivating a trusting relationship is for both parties to prove their trustworthiness to one another. This involves keeping our word at all costs and not doing things that violate trust. Untrustworthy acts are negative inputs that weaken the relationship and hinder growth. What you put into a relationship is what you get out of it. We owe one another love, and cultivating mutual trust is one way we love.

Jesus teaches us this **Kingdom Principle**: A person who can be trusted with a little can also be trusted with much. Prove your trustworthiness in your dating relationship, for example, before you get engaged. And then prove your trustworthiness in your engagement before you get married.

Too often, many people enter into marriages knowing they don't trust those they're marrying. This is a tragedy because trust is essential for a successful relationship.

I'm not saying end the dating relationship if you don't trust the person you're dating. I'm not saying be suspicious while you're dating if your trust is shaky. I'm not saying force the other person to be trustworthy; love is not forceful. What I am saying is the Lord's Word is true. Allow that person time to prove his or her trustworthiness while you're dating before you give him or her all of you in a marriage.

Marriage is an honorable covenant before God, so people entering it should also be honorable. Proving trustworthiness in a relationship should be mutual, so allow yourself time to prove yourself trustworthy, as well.

~Restoring Broken Trust~

Broken trust in a relationship can be restored by what I call the three T's:

(1) Time
(2) Transparency, and
(3) Trustworthiness.

You can restore trust in a relationship if the offending party is willing to prove himself or herself trustworthy and the offended party allows him or her to do so.

If you are the one who violated the trust, re-proving your trustworthiness takes time, so don't rush it. Remain transparent. Don't hide anything. A person who truly desires to restore trust refuses to do the same things over and over again that hurt the other person in the first place.

If your trust has been violated, try not to be skeptical about the other person's actions. Try not to force that person to prove his or her trustworthiness. That should come from a willing heart. Forcing someone to prove trustworthiness puts you into "fight, flight, or freeze" mode and creates unhealthy stress. Instead, pray and trust in God for genuine and lasting change.

Release the other person of his or her faults, and nail them to the past.

By doing these things, over time, both parties will restore the relationship to one of trust, love, and respect.

~Trust In God Working On The Inside Of You~

Believing in the anointing of God working on the inside of you will empower you to accomplish great things. The anointing is inside your heart, so believe in the skills, talents, and abilities He has placed inside you. He didn't put them there to just sit. He put them there because there's something only you can bring to this world.

You were created unique to produce unique greatness. So believe in yourself. Take a step each day. Be patient but diligent. You will reap the success and God will get the glory. 1 Corinthians 15:10 reminds us that God works through us by His grace. Trust in His grace working through you to accomplish great things for His kingdom, your family, and yourself. His grace is more than sufficient.

~Key Takeaways~

- God is worthy of our trust and He trusts in us. We must continue to prove trustworthy with Him and others.
- Learning the many different Names of God teaches you the many different ways God wants you to trust Him.
- Trust must first flow vertically (between you and God) and then horizontally (between you and others).

- Those who trust God don't worry about who they can't trust. They don't spend time and energy worrying about Judas.
- They understand that God protects those who put their trust in Him and that God works all things out for their good.
- The Lord has called us to prove that we are trustworthy in all we do, including the way we conduct our relationships with others.
- A relationship that builds on mutual trust in God and one another becomes a powerful relationship.
- Joy and peace enter through an environment of trust. God can use relationships that are full of trust to accomplish great things for His kingdom.
- Be confident in yourself by trusting in the power of God's anointing work inside of you. That kind of trust can and will help you accomplish many great things. You can do all things through Christ who gives you strength.
- Remember, love thrives in relationships where trust is solid.

Chapter 6

The Powerful Key of Hopefulness

Love…always hopes.
—1 Corinthians 13:7

The God of hope imparts His hope in you when you put your hope in Him. Hope in God is essential to life. It proves our trust in Him; therefore, He supplies us with joy and strength to endure hard times.

Sadly, many people have ended their lives because of hopelessness. Placing hope in things or people while leaving God out is dangerous.

People and circumstances may change, and this can lead to disappointments. In turn, disappointments can lead to all sorts of negative emotions such as bitterness, anger, and depression. Carrying these emotions around with us negatively affects our quality of life and stunts our spiritual growth.

Malachi 3:6, however, assures us that the Lord does not change. Keeping our hope in our unchanging God allows Him to turn disappointments into divine appointments. These divine blessings bring positive emotions such as contentment, joy, and peace, which help us stay free and improves our emotional health.

God's Word makes clear that He is the Source and Giver of hope. Jeremiah 29:11 reminds us of God's promise of hope: "For I know the plans I have for you," declares the Lord, "plans to prosper you and not to harm you, plans to give you **hope** and a future." **Kingdom Principle:** Our part in achieving the future God has for us is to receive our hope from Him by always placing our hope in Him.

~Hope And Faith~

In order for us to exercise faith, we must be hoping for something. Hebrews 11:1 says, "Now faith is confidence in what we **hope** for and assurance about what we do not see." Notice the Scripture says, "What we hope for." So my question to you is, "What are you hoping for?"

~Become A Person Of Great Hope~

People of great hope not only hope for their success now, but also in their lives to come. These people believe in God's promise to prosper and not to harm them. They hope with confidence in God's will being done in their lives because they understand God's will is good and perfect. People of great hope understand that God makes no mistakes. They know He works all things out for their good because they love Him and are called according to His purpose.

If a relationship doesn't last, people of great hope don't allow their love to grow cold because they know God has something much better in store for them. If their bosses lay them off, people of great hope don't give up because they believe God will make a way.

People of great hope don't merely believe for success; they believe the actions they take will lead to that success. People of great hope take the necessary steps to exercise their faith and confidence in God.

~The Priority Of Hope~

Kingdom Principle: People of great hope never hope in anything or anyone more than they do God. Their jobs only bring income, but God is their Source. People of great hope know the earth is the Lord's and the fullness thereof (see Psalm 24:1).

A relationship may bring happiness, but God is the Source of lasting joy and peace. Friends may come and go, but God never leaves nor forsakes.

Our hope should be in God helping us achieve our promotions. Our hope should be in God helping us sustain and build successful relationships. Our hope should be in God working out everything, even what we perceive as bad, for our good. We must have that Daniel type of hope that says, "Regardless of how our God answers, He's still my God and I will forever hope in Him."

Since God's hope is the electricity that runs through our proverbial electrical circuits, we must turn the switch of hope on within our thinking. Draw near to God and receive His hope. He's not out to harm you. He's out to give you hope and a future.

The Love Challenge

In turn, you will be able to share His hope with others. To share hope is to share love. You never know; God might use the hope He provides you to help save a life.

~Hope Brings Emotional And Mental Rest~

Constantly being defensive, anxious, stressed, moody, or irritated is a warning sign of needing emotional and mental rest. The Psalmist David knew exactly what to do during his times of emotional overload. For he said in Psalm 62:5, "Yes, my soul, find **rest** in God; my **hope** comes from him."

Your soul is home to your mind and emotions. When you direct your hope toward God, He gives you hope in return. Notice how the Psalmist said, "My hope comes from him." God's hope brings you into a state of emotional and mental rest.

> *Hope in God and He will give you hope*

Place your hope in Him right now and receive the rest that Jesus promised in Matthew 11:28: "Come to me, all you who are weary and burdened, and I will give you rest."

~God Cares~

Although emotional distress may find us, God doesn't want us to live in it because it places a toll upon our bodies and makes us less effective in life.

When Samuel was grieving over Saul in 1 Samuel 16:1-4, God told him to move on. When Samuel shared his fears with the Lord, the Lord comforted him and gave him the courage and strength to leave his depressed state.

When Elijah was hiding in fear for his life and wanted to die, God told him in 1 Kings 19:3-18 to get up, eat, and move on. Elijah had a hard time regaining his strength, however, because his emotional distress was weighing him down, mentally and physically. Just like Samuel, though, he shared his fears with the Lord, who in turn comforted him and gave him the strength and courage to do as He commanded.

These two great men of God reached a point in their lives where they needed God's comfort and strength to make it through hard times, just as we do today.

We all need God's comfort

God cares about our well-being. He always sends us a word to see us through.

~Hope In God's Word~

While I was stuck in my depression and anxiety, God sent me a word of hope telling me it was time to be healed. So I put my hope in His Word and received that healing. Likewise, when God sent a word of hope to Samuel and Elijah, they placed their hope in it and He strengthened them. Now He's sending you a word of hope through this book.

King David, Samuel, and Elijah all understood this **Kingdom Principle**: Put your hope in God's Word. Psalm 119:114 says, "You are my refuge and my shield; I have put my hope in your word." When you put your hope in God's Word, you place yourself under the protection of His wings. No matter what you go through in life, placing your hope in God's Word, which became flesh, died, and rose again, will elevate you to greater heights.

~Don't Suppress Pain, But Don't Live In It~

Allowing ourselves to suppress or live in emotional distress is unhealthy because it keeps you from going where God's love wants you to go. So acknowledge your emotional pain and cast it upon God in prayer as often as you need to. Tell God exactly how you feel and what you need. He's your Source of comfort, healing, joy, and strength. He will take that pain from you, just like He took it from me and place it on Himself until all of it is gone. He cares. 1 Peter 5:7 says, "Cast all your anxiety on him because he cares for you."

~Jesus' Anguish~

Jesus found Himself in a period of great distress just prior to dying for us. Perhaps the human side of Jesus was thinking about how He would bear our sins and would have to drink the cup of God's wrath. After all, Jesus had never experienced these things before.

Being fully man as well as fully God, Jesus felt many of the same emotions we feel. In the garden of Gethsemane, for example, Jesus acknowledged to His disciples the agony He was experiencing, rather than suppressing it and acting as if nothing was wrong. There's no need for us to pretend there's nothing wrong when it is, so be real with yourself, with those closest to you, and with God the same way Jesus did. He confessed it and prayed, and the Father eventually strengthened Him.

Matthew 26:38 says, "Then he said to them, 'My soul is overwhelmed with sorrow to the point of death. Stay here and keep watch with me.' " When Jesus said, "My soul," He was referring to His inner being. His profound sorrow was affecting Him mentally and emotionally, which also affected Him physically.

Reading about Jesus' experience teaches us that since no one is above Him, all of us may experience some emotional pain at some point. But God is here to help us move past that pain and into strength. Luke 22:43 records that an angel from heaven came to Jesus and strengthened Him. God wants us to rely on Him, His power, and the relief He provides (see 2 Corinthians 1:8-11).

~Emotional Anguish And Your Health~

God created our bodies. He knows that living in long-term emotional distress leads to mental and physical suffering. Even mental health researchers say that remaining in a constant state of emotional distress impairs overall health. God doesn't want us impaired. He wants us to cast our cares upon and put our hope in Him.

Doctors agree that living in emotional distress may cause chronic headaches, muscle tension, inflammation, high blood pressure, and heart disease, along with mental health illnesses such as anxiety and depression.

God came to give us life and more of it. To receive His mercy, grace, compassion, and love is to receive the abundant life He promised. In addition to sharing your pain with those close to you, spend some time in prayer, just as Jesus did during His time of mental anguish. Be real with God about how you feel, and tell Him exactly what you want Him to do about it. Just as He sent Jesus comfort to strengthen Him, God, through Christ, will send you the Comforter to strengthen you.

~Pray And Pray Again~

People of great hope pray for God's will to be done in every situation. Jesus prayed three times for God to remove the cup of suffering from Him. If Jesus prayed more than once about the same thing, we certainly can. At the end of His prayer, He placed His hope in the will of God when He said, "Nevertheless, thy will be done." We should get to the point where we say, "God, if you are willing here's my request, nevertheless my life is in your hands, so your will be done."

~Hope In God's Love~

Love yourself by always directing your hope toward the everlasting love God has for you. Psalm 147:11 tells us, "The Lord delights in those who fear him, who put their **hope** in his unfailing love." Hope in God's love is attached to our reverence for Him. While we should be afraid to be without His love, we should never be afraid to draw near to it. After we place our faith in Jesus, we are in His love; therefore, we have no reason to fear drawing near to God. Being in His perfect love casts out all fear.

~Hope Leads To Joy~

Have you ever wondered why you are not experiencing joy? You are not alone. The Psalmist wondered the same thing. Psalm 42:5 says, "Why, my soul, are you downcast? Why so disturbed within me? Put your **hope** in God, for I will yet praise him, my Savior and my God."

The Psalmist provides us with the solution to joylessness:

(1) Command your emotions to hope in God,
(2) Willfully praise God, and
(3) Remind yourself that He's your Savior and God.

Romans 12:12 reminds us to be joyful in hope.

Hebrews 6:19 teaches us that hope in Christ is the anchor of the soul. An anchor stabilizes things. Hope in Christ brings confidence because it firmly secures and stabilizes you.

Hope in Christ stabilizes your emotions

Those who do not hope in Christ can be defined as unstable in all of their ways (see James 1:8). Those, on the other hand, who make conscious decisions to always hope in the Hope of Glory becomes confident in all of their ways. People of great hope know the Rock is immovable. Placing your hope in God gives you the strength and stability to face some of the most difficult challenges in life, while maintaining your joy.

~Hope And Interpersonal Relationships~

Hope in God takes us out of "fight or flight" mode and places us into emotional stability, thereby helping us cultivate loving relationships. The more we hope in God, the more He restores any chemical imbalances we may have developed from situations that seemed hopeless.

The more chemically balanced we are, the more positive we are. It is the power of the Holy Spirit that increases our joy. And we're able to share that joy with those we are in relationship with.

Emotionally distressed people, on the other hand, transfer that distress to people they're in relationship with. An emotionally distressed husband will transfer his distress to his wife, an emotionally distressed mother will transfer her distress to her children, and an emotionally distressed child will transfer his or her distress to other children. This is a vicious cycle that must be broken.

The only way to break the cycle is to transfer our distress to God instead of other people. He keeps us strong in this life when we cast our weight on Him. Don't worry; He can handle it. Psalm 55:22 says, "Cast your cares on the LORD and he will sustain you; he will never let the righteous be shaken." We are righteous because of faith in the righteousness that Christ provides.

~It's Simple Math~

The attitudes, speech, and behaviors of two people in a relationship will either be positive or negative. Simple addition of positive and negative interactions produces the outcome of any given relationship. What you put into the relationship is what you get out of it. Let's called these inputs. Inputs produce the following three types of relationship outcomes:

1. The Negative Outcome:

Negative input plus negative input equals two negative inputs, so the outcome of this relationship is increased negativity, which is very unhealthy.

2. The Stagnant Outcome:

Positive input plus negative input equals zero. The outcome of this relationship is no growth, so the two of you remain stagnant and get nowhere together.

3. The Positive Outcome:

Positive input plus positive input equals two positive inputs. The outcome of this relationship is growth. This is a healthy relationship where the two of you flourish together!

~God's Positive Love~

God's love is all positive; therefore, in order for us to emit His positive love onto others, we must accept that positive love within our thinking. Never view God or anything He does as negative. Deuteronomy 32:4 says, "He is the Rock, his works are perfect, and all his ways are just. A faithful God who does no wrong, upright and just is he."

Positive thinking about God and our relationship with Him allow that relationship to flourish. God's positive love, working in us, will increase and in turn enable us to cultivate positive and loving relationships with others.

~Loving Others With A Spirit Of Hope~

Hope is the sixth powerful key needed to increase joy, grow spiritually, and build strong relationships. Since we understand that our hope must be in God first and foremost, now we can begin to love others as we love ourselves with what I call a "spirit of hope."

In order to cultivate a spirit of hope, both parties must hope in God. Ephesians 4:4 says, "There is one body and one Spirit, just as you were called to **one hope** when you were called." This one hope creates bonds that cannot be easily broken.

A spirit of hope comes when both parties hope for the success of the relationship. It comes by having a spirit of expectation. It comes by hoping for one another's individual success in life. A spirit of hope comes when each party hopes the other will be all God has called him or her to be.

If your loved one is unsaved, continue to love them by hoping he or she will repent and come to God's love (see 2 Peter 3:9). Don't give up on that person. Instead, continue to pray and thank God in advance for saving him or her.

~Love Yourself With Hope~

Hope for your success. Believe good things can and will happen for you. Don't think or speak your way out of receiving your blessings.

Hope that every action step you take will bring you closer to achieving your dreams. God placed them inside you for a reason, so don't let them die there. The world needs what you have to offer. Keep hoping while dedicating all you do for the glory of God.

Proverbs 13:12 says, "Hope deferred makes the heart sick, but a longing fulfilled is a tree of life." In other words, don't put off what you're hoping for. Go after it. If you desire a better relationship with your child, go after it. If you desire a better marriage, don't put it off.

> *Go after what you're hoping for*

Work on it today. If you desire your own business, work a little each day. Begin right where you are. Do what you can and God will do what you can't.

Jesus gives us this **Kingdom Principle** in Matthew 7:7: We must do the asking, seeking, and knocking. If we are not afraid to ask, He'll allow us to receive whatever He wills for our lives. If we take a step of faith and start seeking, God will allow us to find the way. If we start knocking, He'll open the doors of opportunity. Lamentations 3:25 says, "The LORD is good to those whose hope is in him, to the one who seeks him."

~Key Takeaways~

- The God of hope gives us real and lasting hope when we place our hope in Him.
- God is good to those who place their hope in Him.
- We need faith in order to please God, and we need hope in order to have faith. Faith has no substance if there's no hope.
- People of great hope never hope in anything or anyone more than they hope in God.
- Hope in God anchors the emotions. It leads to mental and emotional stability, which increases our mental, physical, and spiritual health.
- People of great hope place their hope in God working through them and others to cultivate loving relationships.
- People of great hope place their hope in God working in them to accomplish their goals.
- People of great hope always hope for the salvation and success of their loved ones as well as themselves.
- Friends, love always hopes.

Chapter 7

The Powerful Key of Persevering

> Love…always perseveres.
> —1 Corinthians 13:7

God displays His love toward us through the power of His perseverance. He's a holy God, yet He endures with us, even through some of our most rebellious times. Even when He knocked on the doors of our hearts, and we didn't let Him in, He gave us another opportunity to open the door and accept His love.

Even when we insult His presence with sin, He doesn't cast us out. Instead, He releases new mercies and gives us time to get things right. In spite of our unfaithfulness, He remained faithful.

He didn't leave us in the blindness of our own self-righteousness. Instead, He gave us the spiritual sight to see His righteousness through Christ. God won't give up on His elect, for Hebrews 13:5 says He'll never leave us or forsake us. So don't give up on Him, don't give up on yourself, and don't give up on your loved ones.

~Jesus' Perseverance~

Imagine coming into a world that you created only to be rejected, unappreciated, accused, mocked, betrayed, denied, punished, and killed for the sins committed against you. Jesus willfully endured all these things.

Love is an action, not merely a feeling. The man side of Jesus wasn't feeling the cup of suffering. In fact, the Gospels record that He asked the Father three times to take the cup away from Him.

Even though the Gospels don't record Jesus receiving an answer from the Father, He didn't give up on Him, and He didn't give up on us. Instead, He emptied Himself, relied on the power of the Father, and willfully drank the cup out of love for His Father first and us second.

> *Jesus didn't give up*

~It Didn't Look So Good~

To the human eye, it didn't look as if God's plan on Calvary was going to succeed, as Mark 15:31 tells us the chief priests and teachers of the law mocked Jesus: "He saved others, but he can't save himself!" Jesus was derided, spit on, whipped, and crucified. To the human eye, therefore, it looked as if all hope was gone for our King.

We know, however, that God's plan did work and it is working now. Look at the billions of people who have become believers worldwide because of one Man's perseverance.

~Perseverance, Faith, And Spiritual Sight~

We walk not by our physical sight but by faith in God, which leads to the next **Kingdom Principle**: We are not walking around blind or clueless because our faith is our sight. Our spiritual sight allows us to tap into the supernatural and endure adversity in every area of our lives.

The Apostle Paul wrote about our spiritual sight in the Book of Hebrews. Referring to Moses, Hebrews 11:27 says, "By faith he left Egypt, not fearing the king's anger; he persevered because he saw him who is invisible."

Moses saw God even though he didn't see God. This is spiritual sight. Despite the threats of a dangerous king, Moses' spiritual sight and faith helped him keep his focus on the "King" with a big "K" so he wouldn't fear what the "king" with a little "k" would do.

You and I have spiritual sight because the Spirit of God is leading us and it doesn't get any better than that. God will never lead His children astray. Romans 8:14 says, "For those who are led by the Spirit of God are the children of God." We must, therefore, keep our focus on God and not our circumstances.

> Your faith is your spiritual sight

The Spirit of God places a snapshot of the "big picture" inside our hearts. Our part is to believe what God has revealed to our spirit and take the steps He orders us to take.

To the human eye, our lives may not look like the picture God showed us in our spirit. This is normal. God is working things out in the Spiritual realm before they come to pass in the earthly realm. This leads us to our next **Kingdom Principle**: Don't depend on your physical sight; walk by your spiritual sight by depending on God's Word and His promises. Stay focused on the big picture.

If God said your relationship will recover, even if it doesn't look as if it will, see it as restored. If God said your children will be saved even though they're in the world, see them as saved. If God said you're going to be successful, even if your situation looks defeated, see yourself as successful. Believe in God's Word because it is true.

~Speaking To Negativity~

The older generation of Israelites didn't receive the promises of God because they didn't believe in what God had said. In Numbers 13:2, God commanded Moses to send 12 men to explore the Promised Land. After their 40-day journey, 10 of the 12 returned with bad reports, even though God had already promised them the land back in Leviticus. Yet only two believed what God had said. The **Kingdom Principle** to be learned here is: Nothing angers God more than unbelief in what He says. God is not a man to lie.

The older generation Israelites didn't believe because they walked by their physical sight instead of their spiritual sight. They focused on themselves and their circumstances, which gave them a negative spirit.

Their negative outlook led to negative speaking, which made them want to give up. So essentially, they talked themselves out of receiving their blessing. They said, "We can't do it. Our obstacles are more powerful and stronger than we are. We look like grasshoppers in our own eyes and in the eyes of our giants." Are you talking yourself out of receiving God's blessings?

These people made three grave mistakes:

(1) They saw themselves as small and their obstacles as big, when they should have been looking at their big and powerful God.
(2) They worried about the way others saw them instead of believing in what God had said about them.
(3) They spoke death into their lives when they said in Numbers 14:2, "...Only if we had died in Egypt! Or in this wilderness!"

They allowed what they saw to discourage them to the point of giving up on themselves, one another, and God.

Joshua and Caleb, on the other hand, believed because they focused on what God had said. They silenced those negative voices by speaking back to them: "We can do it." Even when the negative voices came back stronger and frustrated them, Numbers 14:7 records that they spoke with more intensity by repeating what God had said. Remember, God always has the final say.

What are you saying to the negative voices that play within your mind? Remember this **Kingdom Principle**: Always speak against them by declaring what God has said. God declared the land was good, and Joshua and Caleb, walking by their spiritual sight, declared the same thing. The point is to see things the way God speaks them and declare what God has spoken to your heart.

Declare to the negativity in your life, "I can do it!" "My body is whole and sustained by God's favor"; "My relationship is restored and full of love"; "My book is in bookstores, successful and changing lives"; "My fashion design business is open and flourishing." Focus on what God said you can do and take the necessary steps to get there.

Joshua and Caleb declared God's Word and focused on what they could do by God's grace (see Numbers 14:8). They understood if God was for them, nothing or no one could stand against them. They spoke against the negative voices and unbelief, which eventually died by the fruit of their own words. As a result of their "can do" spirit, they pleased God and received His promises. They simply had a different spirit from those who didn't believe (see Numbers 14:24).

Dare to be different. Dare to stay positive. Don't see yourself as insignificant. God created you to be greater than you know. Don't assume you know how other people see you. It doesn't matter anyway because God sees you as capable and mighty.

Don't worry about your obstacles because God is bigger than anything you may face. God has designed every obstacle to be a stepping stool to help elevate you to the next level of faith.

Maintaining this type of tenacity allows you to endure and obtain what others may see and believe to be impossible. Mark 9:23 reminds us of Jesus' declaration that everything is possible for the one who believes.

~Perseverance And Desire~

There's another component to endurance, which is desire. Desiring to see God's will done in your life keeps your heart burning like a flame. Jesus taught us to pray, "Thy will be done on earth as it is in heaven." Pray for God's will to be done in your life and desire to see it come to pass. It will happen.

~Persevering In God's Will~

Jesus persevered in doing God's will. As followers of Christ, we are called to only persevere in what God has called us to endure. Hebrews 10:36 says, "You need to persevere so that when you have done the will of God, you will receive what he has promised." This applies to every area of our lives.

We stay in the will of God by:

(1) Refusing to love money,
(2) Maintaining sexual morality,
(3) Hating deceit,
(4) Staying away from greed, and
(5) Staying humble.

Many of us are bearing people, emotions, and situations that God has not called us to bear. Enduring things outside of God's will is destructive and counterproductive to being about the Father's business.

Persevering in relationships, emotions, and situations outside of God's will destroys us mentally, physically, and spiritually. Some believers are enduring the curse of the law because of incorrect teaching. Others are enduring bondage, thinking they cannot remarry because of false doctrine (see 1 Timothy 4:1-3).

Where the Spirit of the Lord is there is liberty to serve God and others in love and with a pure heart and a clean conscience, not bondage to damaging relationships, false teaching, or a life under the law.

~Perseverance And Joy~

Another reason Jesus was able to persevere during times of adversity is because He looked ahead. Jesus walked with the big picture in mind. He talked with the big picture in mind. He saw you, me, and many others saved. He saw us added to the kingdom of heaven because God worked through Him. He saw the glory He would share with the Father in the future. These things gave Him great joy.

As followers of Christ, we are called to endure our own race as Christ endured His. In Hebrews 12:2, the Apostle Paul gave us the key to running our race with endurance: "Fixing our eyes on Jesus, the pioneer and perfecter of faith. For the joy set before him he endured the cross, scorning its shame, and sat down at the right hand of the throne of God."

As we focus our spiritual sight on Jesus, He strengthens us and gives us joy. He helps us achieve a mental focus, which cannot be achieved through human logic. The human eye can only see the long road ahead with all its obstacles.

Just because we're human, we might find ourselves thinking ourselves out of running the race God has set before us. We will tell ourselves things like, "It's too hard," or "I can't do it." We persevere, however, by keeping our focus on God's Word, which enables us to keep moving toward victory inside our homes and churches in spite of the many obstacles, adversities, and oppositions we may face.

Don't give up. Joy lies ahead. Every victory brings joy and the endurance will be well worth it. We're not running by ourselves. Jesus is ahead, offering us the living waters of His Spirit, motivating us to run the best race we can. We must reach out, accept His cup of help, and drink. It is Christ who gives you strength to endure.

Joy comes in the morning

~A Lesson In Perseverance From Nick~

Nick Vujicic was born without limbs. In spite of his differences, Nick's parents did their very best to forward him every opportunity to live what many call a normal life. Unbeknownst to them, however, Nick was born to live an extraordinary life.

When Nick was young, his parents allowed him to attend mainstream schooling. He began to perceive the challenges of having no arms and no legs while most kids his age were learning to do things for themselves. Because of his physical challenges, young Nick also faced being ridiculed and bullied, as well as his own inability to see a bright future for himself. As a result, Nick spiraled into low self-esteem and spells of depression. He began to feel lonely and often wondered if there was anyone else like him and if there was any other purpose for living other than to feel misfortune and pain. At the tender age of ten, Nick attempted suicide in a tub of water. Thinking about his parents; however, he didn't go through with it.

As time went on, Nick became angry with God and refused to serve Him without knowing why he was born without limbs. Little did Nick know, God had a great purpose for His life.

At the age of fifteen, Nick placed his faith in Jesus after reading John 9. Taking one day at a time, Nick began to discover

The Love Challenge

God's purpose and plan for his life. Together, God and his family helped him endure his depression, low self-esteem, and fear.

Nick's parents taught him a valuable truth I believe is worth repeating. "You have two choices," they said. "You can either be angry for what you don't have, or be thankful for what you do have." They also told Nick, "Do your best, and God will do the rest." These golden nuggets still speak truth to his heart to this day.

Without perseverance, God would have never used Nick at the of age seventeen, to start a non-profit organization called Life Without Limbs, which brings people to the love of God found in Christ.

Without perseverance, God would have never used Nick to inspire millions of teens and adults at more than 2,000 speaking engagements in more than 50 countries. If Nick would have given up, God would have never used him and his ministry to lead more than 200,000 souls to Jesus.

Without perseverance, God would have never used Nick to write four books, one of which was translated into 27 different languages and continues to bless and inspired the lives of many. Nick's faith in God allowed him to persevere in spite of his physical limitations and do what many believe was impossible. Friends, this is the power of perseverance.

If you like to know more about Nick's ministry *Life Without Limbs* or provide support, please visit www.lifewithoutlimbs.org

~Persevering In Love With Others~

Persevering with others comes from a love that says, "I'm not giving up on you!" Persevering is maintaining a sense of purpose and continuing to walk toward that purpose, in spite of difficulties, obstacles, or discouragement. Perseverance is the seventh powerful key needed to increase joy, grow spiritually, and build strong relationships.

When the going gets tough, many people give up too easily. Instead of marching up the mountain to reach greatness, they go around it just to find another one on the other side. They keep looking for the easy way out while getting nowhere. The reality is there's no easy way to success. A person who avoids the endurance and work required to go up the mountain will never reach the top.

Eliminating alternatives is the key to persevering with others in love. Many relationships, especially marriages, are rocky because of alternatives. Success should be the only option in relationships where people are willing to work.

> *Success is the only option*

Motivating his men, a Marine Colonel once said, "We are surrounded. That simplifies the problem." Because the Colonel saw no other alternatives, he was not distracted or double minded. He and his team, therefore, could focus on a single objective: winning.

When your back is against the rope and you want to survive, the only way out is to fight. Fight for your relationships. Fight for your marriage. Fight for your children. Having no other alternatives but to succeed helps you develop and maintain a mindset and sense of purpose needed to win.

2 Thessalonians 3:5 says, "May the Lord direct your hearts into God's love and Christ's perseverance." Paul prayed for God to direct his people hearts into Christ's perseverance. You and I can do the same thing. Pray for the hearts of the ones you love. Pray they don't give up on you, God, nor themselves. God is the only One capable of touching them. However, he may touch them through you. Perseverance allows you to create strong, genuine, and meaningful relationships.

~Persevere With Yourself~

If you constantly give up, don't expect to produce or grow anything. You have Christ inside you; thus, you are well capable of completing what you start.

What most people perceive to be failures are merely opportunities to learn and bounce back stronger. Adversity builds character if properly handled with an enduring mindset that says, "I'm not giving up."

Don't die with your visions. Be determined to see them fulfilled. God placed those visions inside your heart to be birth by you. Be confident. Write your vision down. Read it daily and run toward it with diligence. Leave your legacy.

Encourage yourself. Get some rest. Always spend some alone time with God in prayer to gather strength to endure.

Remember this **Kingdom Principle**: There are rewards attached to persevering. Galatians 6:9 says, "Let us not become weary in doing good, for at the proper time we will reap a harvest if we do not give up." So don't grow tired in your love for others. Don't grow tired with yourself. Don't grow tired doing God's will. Your harvest is on the way!

~Key Takeaways~

- God perseveres with you. He said He'll never leave you nor forsake you.
- Don't give up on God. Trust His Word. Walk by your spiritual sight, not your physical sight. God placed the vision in your heart to be fulfilled. Do your part.
- Have a burning desire and the patience to see God's will fulfilled in your life. Your reward will be great.
- Don't put additional weight on yourself. Endure in God's will only. Depend on His power working through you.
- Run your best race at your own pace. Never compare yourself to others.
- Know God's purpose for your relationships. Have a purpose for everything you do. Purpose keeps you driving.
- Endure with others in love as they endure with you.
- Friends, love endures.

Chapter 8

The Powerful Key of Unfailing Love

> Love never fails.
> —1 Corinthians 13:8

This is how much God loves you: He commanded part of Him to die so you could live with Him. God is love and defines what love is. 1 John 4:10 says, "**This is love:** not that we loved God, but that he loved us and sent his Son as an atoning sacrifice for our sins."

1 John 4:10 defines love as:

(1) God loving you,
(2) God sending Jesus to die in your place, and
(3) Jesus paying the debt for your sins.

If you look closely at these three points, you'll see all of God's loving attributes. You'll see how patient, kind, unselfish, forgiving, slow to anger, protective, trusting, hopeful, longsuffering, and reliable God's love is. There's no love like His.

~Be Mindful Of God's Love~

The Psalmist teaches us this **Kingdom Principle**: Always be mindful of God's love. Always think about how reliable His love has been toward you. Psalm 26:3 says, "For I have always been **mindful** of your **unfailing love** and have lived in reliance on your faithfulness."

This Scripture is a Psalm of King David. We know David was not perfect. Neither are we. David made some mistakes. So do we. Nevertheless, he kept his mind on God's unfailing love for him, which he knew he didn't deserve and he didn't take it for granted. But he also didn't live in fear or condemnation because of the unfaithful acts he committed. Instead, he repented and lived in reliance on God's faithfulness.

Scholars refer to the Psalms as "Wisdom Literature." Wisdom is applying what Scripture teaches to our lives. Psalm 26:3 teaches us it is wise to always be aware or mindful of God's love.

Be aware of how God has kept you from harm and death. Even though the weapon formed, it didn't kill you. Also be aware of how He's keeping you now, fighting battles both seen and unseen. Be aware of how His love sustains your life. He provides for all your needs.

1 Corinthians 1:9 says, "God is faithful, who has called you into fellowship with his Son, Jesus Christ our Lord." Hebrews 11:6 reminds us that faith pleases God and He rewards us according to our belief. Relying on God's faithfulness is a wise act of faith that pleases Him.

~Know It, Trust It, And Live In It~

1 John 4:16 says, "And so we know and rely on the love God has for us. God is love. Whoever lives in love lives in God, and God in them." We must be confident in the love God has for us. Know it! Trust it! Live in it!

Exodus 15:13 reminds us that God's love will lead us into eternal salvation. Romans 8:14 says, "For those who are led by the Spirit of God are the children of God." Since God is love, I believe it is safe to say, "those who are led by the Spirit of **Love** are the children of **Love**." Those who are led by God's Spirit of love are those who:

(1) Know God's love,
(2) Trust in God's love, and
(3) Live in God's love.

~There's No Fear In Love~

1 John 4:18 teaches us those who fear for their salvation are not fully experiencing God's love. People with such fear have not fully accepted that Jesus received their punishment on Calvary.

These people have not accepted that their sins have been nailed to the cross and that they are in God's love. Being in God's love through Christ removes fear of punishment.

We are now free, not free to live old lives, but free to live new lives in God's love. You are free to become who God created you to be. You are free to serve and love God with a clear mind. You are free to love others and yourself with a pure heart. Unfailing love is the eighth powerful key needed to increase joy, grow spiritually, and build strong relationships.

~Faith Is The Seed~

Your faith is the seed that firmly plants you into God's soil of love. Once you are firmly established in Christ's love, within your mind, heart, and emotions, you will be able to sprout and begin to experience His love to a greater extent.

Experiencing God's limitless love is an ongoing process. We will experience all His love when Christ returns to present us before Him. Meanwhile, our faith is the seed that pushes us deeper into His soil of love. As we experience it by faith, we grow and continue to produce more evidence of being in God, which is increased love for others.

Galatians 5:6 reminds us that faith expresses itself through love. Our Lord reminds us in John 13:35 that, "By this everyone will know that you are my disciples, if you love one another." Love is our mark of being in God; it is our mark of being a disciple of Christ.

> Faith conveys itself through love

~The Fruit Of Love~

Galatians 5:22 reminds us that love is a fruit of the Spirit. We cannot self-generate godly love. Since we started by faith, we must continue in faith. John 15:5 says, "I am the vine; you are the branches. If you remain in me and I in you, you will bear much fruit; apart from me you can do nothing." Our connection to Christ's love by faith allows us to bear much fruit of love for Him, others, and ourselves.

1 John 4:7 reminds us that love comes from God. We are simply channels of God's love. But in order to be channels, we must stay connected to the Vine. This connection takes place within our heart, mind, and emotions. We're able to love Him, others, and ourselves when we know with all our heart, mind, and emotions, that He first loved us.

~What God Has Joined~

God is the Origin of love and the Source that sustains it. If you are in Christ by faith, you are forever connected to God's love. Romans 8:38-39 declares that nothing will ever separate us from the love of God displayed through Christ—not a flaw, not a person, not a devil, not a mistake—nothing!

1 Corinthians 6:17 says, "But whoever is united with the Lord is one with him in spirit." Never see yourself disconnected from God, because "as a person thinks in their heart, so is he or she." If you believe within your heart that you are disconnected, you will feel disconnected. If you believe within your heart that you are connected, because the Word of Truth declares that you are, you will feel connected.

This connection with Christ will continue to strengthen and empower you to experience and share His love with others. Your cup of love will overflow because you'll have the love of God pouring into you.

~Closing The Umbrellas~

Picture God's love, including all its attributes in 1 Corinthians 13:4-8, raining down upon you. Now picture yourself opening your umbrella and lifting it over your head. Do you see what's happening? His love is still directed towards you, but your umbrella is blocking it from touching you.

Perhaps your umbrella is living in guilt and condemnation. Perhaps your umbrella is being afraid to dedicate your life to Him just as you are. Perhaps your umbrella is holding up hopelessness. Perhaps your umbrella is living in fear and anxiety. Whatever your umbrella may be, bring it down and close it! God wants to pour His love on you. Don't block it. Let His unfailing love rain down on you. His love cleanses. His love nourishes. His love gives life. His love grows. It strengthens. It empowers you. Receive it!

~Maturing In God's Love~

In Ephesians 3:14-20, the Apostle Paul prays for God to develop and strengthen the body of believers in Ephesus. He prays for their thinking. He prays they will be able to grasp within their mind how limitless Christ's love is.

In his prayer, he mentions that every believer should have a basic understanding of how great the love of God is. Although Christ's love is too great for anyone to fully understand, Paul prays they would allow themselves to experience it, and as a result, grow spiritually in God.

This prayer teaches us that all believers should know there's no limit to God's love. We only limit ourselves from experiencing it when we walk away or hold up mental umbrellas such as condemnation.

> Don't limit God's love

Embracing His love within our hearts and allowing it to rain down on our minds enables us to mature spiritually in God. One day, we will experience the fullness of God's love in eternity. Today, let's embrace and enjoy the fact that He loves us now.

~A New Covenant~

When God established the Old Covenant with His chosen people, He instructed Moses, the mediator, to proclaim His commands to the people. He then sprinkled the commandments and the people with the blood of animals, along with water. Their sins were forgiven, they were washed clean, and they agreed to keep God's commands. This confirmed the covenant God made with them.

It's important to note that no one forced them to receive this. They received it by faith. In addition, this covenant could not permanently take away sins nor give eternal life. It was only a copy of the new and improved covenant that would come.

When God established His New Covenant, Jesus, the mediator, proclaimed God's commandments to His people, just like Moses did. Christ then offered Himself as a one-time sacrifice to God on Calvary to take away sin once and for all.

When you profess Jesus as your Lord and Savior from the heart, Christ sprinkles your heart with His blood. You are now washed by the Word and the Spirit of God, who gives you new life. As a result, you stand before God forgiven and clean.

Jesus reminds us in John 13:8 that He must wash us for us to be saved. Even though many of us may feel unworthy like Peter did, in order to become one with God, we must receive the washing of Jesus and His grace by faith.

Romans 11:27 says, "And this is my covenant with them when I take away their sins." Revelation 1:5 reads, "And from Jesus Christ, who is the faithful witness, the firstborn from the dead, and the ruler of the kings of the earth. To him who loves us and has freed us from our sins by his blood."

Our part of the New Covenant is to fulfill God's commands. We do so by living a new life of love and seeing ourselves as God calls us.

When we receive Christ, God calls us by new names. He calls us holy. He calls us His children. He calls us His disciples. He calls us friends. He calls us new creations. He calls us beloved. He calls us His righteous, not because of what we do or have done, but because of what God has done through Christ. Our part is to answer the call and become who He has called us to be.

~A New Command~

With the New Covenant came a "New Command." John 13:34-35 says, "**A new command** I give you: Love one another. As I have loved you, so you must love one another. By this everyone will know that you are my disciples, if you love one another." Why is this a new command? God has always commanded love. I suggest it's a new command because in Christ, God has given us the ability to live it out. It's a new command because we are under a New Covenant of grace. It's a new command because God gave us new hearts and new spirits according to the Old Testament prophecy in Ezekiel 36:26, and the New Testament explanation of that prophecy given by the Apostle Paul in Hebrews 10:16.

The New Covenant could not go into effect without Jesus shedding His blood. Paul draws a parallel between the Old Covenant and the New Covenant in Hebrews 9:18: "This is why even the first covenant was not put into effect without blood."

There's life in the blood of Jesus. As soon as we open our hearts to Him, He sprinkles His blood on them and shares His life with us. We then become New Covenant believers with new lives because of His bloodshed. Luke 22:20 says, "In the same way, after the supper he took the cup, saying, "This cup is the new covenant in my blood, which is poured out for you."

What's also new about the command to "love one another" is Christ has set the example. He gave us His Spirit to empower us to fulfill His command, which is to, "Love one another. As I have loved you."

~Loving God~

We must love God more than ourselves, possessions, and others. 2 Chronicles 16:9 reminds us that the eyes of God searches the earth to strengthen those whose hearts are fully committed to Him.

God does not measure our love for Him by our words or how we feel. He measures our love for Him by our acts of obedience from the heart. Jesus loved the Father first, and then us by His actions, regardless of how difficult it

> **Fully commit your heart to God**

was for Him to die in the flesh for our sins. Nevertheless, He obeyed and the Father raised Him to life.

When we obey by believing the Word of Truth, God raises us to life with Christ. As our Lord, He expects us to love Him through our actions, and crucify our flesh regardless of how difficult it may be.

Jesus tells us in John 14:15, "If you love me, keep my commands," which He gives us in John 15:12: "My command is this: Love each other as I have loved you."

Even though this appears to be one command, in Matthew 22:36-39, Jesus actually gives us two: (1) love God, and (2) love others. Our love for others, out of our love for God, fulfills our love for Him. This is likely the reason why Jesus only mentions one command, even though He says "commands."

In Matthew 22:40, Jesus tells us "All the Law and the Prophets hang on these two commandments." In other words, all of the "thou shalt not's" and the "do's" of the Bible are based on (1) loving God and (2) loving others.

Every time we refuse to harm someone else, we prove our love for God. Every time we overcome a "thou shalt not," we show God we love Him. The mere fact that we fight to keep the "do's" and fight to stay away from the "don'ts" is proof that God is our Treasure.

Keep fighting and don't give up. You will overcome the areas in your life that have been affected by sin and conquer new territory for God. God will tell you which areas He wants you to conquer, and when you conquer those areas, you will increase your territory. God calls you more than a conqueror. He calls you mighty. Continue to become what He called you to be.

~Loved As Friends~

Romans 5:8 tells us that God, through Christ, loved us even when we were sinners. Romans 5:10 tells us to love our enemies because He loved us as enemies. He now loves us as friends and tells us to abide in His love as friends.

Jesus says in John 15:14, "You are my friends **if** you do what I command." The word **"if"** puts a condition on us staying in the love of Christ as friends.

Jesus teaches us that we abide in His love as friends by keeping His commands. The word "keep" in the Greek language is *tēreō*, which means to properly maintain, observe, preserve, spiritually guard, watch over, and keep intact. This is what we are to do with God's commands to love Him and others because sin, situations, and Satan will challenge our obedience.

Jesus teaches us in Matthew 24:10-12 that there will come a time that many will depart from the faith and hate others because of false teaching, betrayal, sin, and their love growing cold. If we keep paying our covenant debt of love, however, we will not depart from the faith and we will abide in His love as friends. In Matthew 24:13 Jesus says, "But the one who stands firm to the end will be saved."

God takes the word "friend" very seriously, so seriously that He sent His Son to lay down His life for His friends. He also says in Proverbs 17:17 that a friend loves at all times and in Proverbs 18:24 that there's a friend who sticks closer than a brother.

Obedience is required. Jesus asks in Luke 6:46, "Why do you call me, 'Lord, Lord,' and do not do what I say?" The Lord also tells us in John 15:10, "If you keep my commands, you will remain in my love, just as I have kept my Father's commands and remain in his love."

Notice what Jesus said: "Just as I have **kept** my Father's commands and remain in His love." If Jesus had to obey His debt of love by laying down His life, we must also obey our debt of love and lay down our lives to live for God.

God's commands are very important to Him, a fact He reveals from Genesis to Revelation; therefore, His commands should be equally important to us. They protect us from hurt, harm, danger, and death associated with departing from the faith. A person who understands the protective nature of God's commands is never satisfied with breaking any of them.

Our obedience must come from a heart made soft by the Holy Spirit. This kind of heart stands before God as loved and forgiven because of Christ, desires to abide in God's love as a friend, and cherishes the friendship. The more we fight to "keep" God's precious commands, the better we become at it. It's a process, one that yields great results and rewards.

John 15:15-16 reveals to us the benefits of abiding in God's love as His friends:

(1) Knowing God's will,
(2) Bearing plenty of fruit for God's Kingdom that will last, and
(3) Our prayers being answered.

Deuteronomy 12:28 reminds us to, "Be careful to obey all these regulations I am giving you, so that it may always go well with you and your children after you, because you will be doing what is good and right in the eyes of the LORD your God!"

~God Sets The Example~

Ephesians 5:1-2 says, "Follow God's example, therefore, as dearly loved children and walk in the way of love, just as Christ loved us and gave himself up for us as a fragrant offering and sacrifice to God." We must accept that we are dearly loved by God in order to follow His example of loving dearly.

> *Follow God's example of love*

Jesus loved us as Himself. Unless we embrace this fact, it's going to be difficult for us to follow His example. Unless we understand and embrace how God has loved us, it's going to be difficult for us to love others His way. Unless we understand that God is the **Source** of our love for others, it's going to be hard for us to walk in His way of love. Exercising Biblical love for others proves our connection with Him and shows our love for Him.

1 Corinthians 14:1 calls us to follow the way of love. God, through Christ, is that Way. In order to love others by following His example, we must first know His loving ways. I call these the "loving attributes of God." 1 John 4:18 says, "We love because he first loved us," and because of that, we are now empowered by the Holy Spirit to love others according to His Word.

~Loving From A Pure Heart~

Before we go into the loving attributes of God, I must say this **Kingdom Principle**: Sincere love comes from a pure heart. Jesus reminds us in Matthew 5:8 that, "Blessed are the pure in heart, for they

> *Love for others comes from a pure heart*

will see God." Acts 15:9 teaches us that our hearts are purified by faith. 1 Peter 1:22 reminds us, "Now that you have purified yourselves by obeying the truth so that you have sincere love for each other, love one another deeply, from the heart."

Obeying the Word of Truth is believing that God, through Christ, has purified us. Accepting this truth is knowing without a doubt that we have been purified by the blood of Jesus alone! This type of unwavering faith is essential to operating in the type of freedom that allows us to love others from a pure and sincere heart.

It is our responsibility to guard our hearts and keep them free from defilement by removing anything from them that is not like God. This type of purification enables us to continue to love from a pure heart.

~The Loving Attributes Of God~

Now that we know the blood of Jesus has made our hearts pure, let's discuss God's loving attributes as seen in 1 Corinthians 13:4-8. As I list these attributes, I want you to think about whether you view God the way they describe Him. Think about how He expresses His love for you through each attribute.

2 Corinthians 13:5 reminds us to examine ourselves to see if we're in the faith. We know that faith shows up in love. As you read the list, measure how well you exhibit these loving attributes in all of your relationships.

Lastly, understand that God is the only One who loves perfectly. Please take that into account and allow yourself and others room to mature in these attributes, not by force, but by faith, truth, mutual accountability, and obedience to the Spirit of God pressing upon our hearts to exercise them out of Biblical love toward others each day.

God is love and 1 Corinthians 13:4-8 defines love as being:

(1) Patient,
(2) Kind,
(3) Forgiving,
(4) Protecting,
(5) Trusting,
(6) Hopeful,
(7) Persevering, and
(8) Unfailing.

Look closely at each attribute on this list and you'll see God, through Christ, in every single one of them.

God is very patient with you. He's slow to anger, He saved you through His kindness, and He forgives and releases all of your sins. When you confess, Christ covers. He protects you. Your salvation is secured by His mighty hand. He's trustworthy and places His trust in you. He has never told you a lie. He's the God of hope. He gives you hope. He perseveres with you through all your rebelliousness and adversity. He said He'll never leave you nor forsake you. His love is unfailing. Our Lord God is faithful.

~Loving Others With These Attributes~

God calls us to express love by exhibiting these eight attributes of Biblical love toward others. Out of our love for God, we make every effort to follow His example from a heart that is pure and loved by Him.

The Holy Spirit is at work producing these eight loving attributes in us. Our part is to recognize when He's at work in our lives and submit to His leading by obeying. Isaiah 64:8 says, "Yet you, LORD, are our Father. We are the clay, you are the potter; we are all the work of your hand." God is still at work in all of us. He's reshaping us from the fallen Adam to take on the characteristics of the risen Christ.

Knowing these eight attributes of love and perceiving how God extends them toward you each day will help you love others the way He has loved you. By expressing these loving attributes daily, we'll cultivate loving homes, relationships, and churches.

Embracing that God is and has been patient with you puts you in the right mindset to become more patient. Embracing the fact that God is kind toward you, will help you become more kind toward others. Embracing that God forgives you and does not hold your sins over your head will help you forgive others and not hold their sins against them.

Embracing the fact that God endures with you in love will help you endure with others. Embracing that God trusts you and wants you to prove trustworthy will help you cultivate trusting relationships. Embracing that God places His hope in you will allow you to hope for others as well as yourself. Understanding that God's love never fails will help you to never fail to love.

~Love And Joy~

Love is connected to the joy of the Lord. Developing a tenacious spirit of love produces joy, which comes from God alone. Nevertheless, life teaches us that trials and tribulations may try to rob us of our joy.

Since God is our supplier of joy, we must request a resupply from Him to help us bear the times of testing. Satan is present during these times because our struggle is not with flesh and blood. He wants to kill, steal, and destroy. In other words, he wants you to give up. He understands the joy of the Lord is your strength. He works overtime to try to make your love grow cold. If you allow him to cause your love to grow cold, he steals your joy. If he steals your joy, he steals your strength. And if he depletes your strength, you might quit. Don't quit! The devil is a liar! The anointing inside of you is greater than he is, so don't let him have your strength. Instead, ask God for more joy. Psalm 86:4 says, "Bring joy to your servant, Lord, for I put my trust in you."

> Pray for a resupply of God's joy

~See Yourself As Love~

Your body is the temple of the Holy Spirit and the Holy Spirit is love; therefore, you are love on legs. Let your walk be a walk of love. Let your talk be a talk of love. Let your actions be actions of love. See God's love raining down on you. See yourself as an embodiment of His love. He has accepted you because of Christ, so believe that you are absolutely loved by Him. Be affirmed in His love and watch how it matures and strengthens you.

> See yourself as love

~Growing In Love~

Love is a fruit of the Spirit, and He is the Source we draw love from, thereby increasing the love in us. 1 Thessalonians 3:12 says, "May the Lord make your love increase and overflow for each other and for everyone else, just as ours does for you."

Pray often for God to increase love within every heart you are connected to, including your own. Faith without works is dead. While relying on God's love, we must do our part and love one another.

~Accountability Is Love~

Loving others also means holding others accountable. Failing to discipline a child, for example, is unloving. Proverbs 13:24 reminds us that a parent who loves his or her children disciplines them. God disciplines those He loves.

Not holding someone accountable to the law that protects people from harm is also unloving. Not speaking up against a clear injustice, within your circle of influence, is also unloving. In Micah 6:8, God called us to act justly – to love truth and hate wrong.

To hold others and ourselves accountable is an act of love. James 5:20 says, "Remember this: Whoever turns a sinner from the error of their way will save them from death and cover over a multitude of sins." 1 Peter 4:8 says, "Above all, love each other deeply, because love covers over a multitude of sin." One way to love each other deeply and cover over a multitude of sins, is to hold one another accountable. Ephesians 5:21 says, "Submit to one another out of reverence for Christ."

In Galatians 2:11-13, Paul mentions how he confronted Peter face to face about his wrongful treatment and hypocrisy towards the Gentiles, which was leading other believers astray. Love calls a spade a spade, but it does so with a spirit of restoration, not condemnation.

~Loving From A Distance~

Mark 10 records a rich young man who ran to Jesus, knelt before Him, and asked, "What must I do to inherit eternal life?" Jesus tells him that he knows the commandments, after which the rich young man declares that he has kept all of the commandments since he was a boy.

Mark 10:21 says, "Jesus looked at him and loved him. "One thing you lack," he said. "Go, sell everything you have and give to the poor, and you will have treasure in heaven. Then come, follow me." Verse 22 says, "At this the man's face fell. He went away sad, because he had great wealth."

Notice how verse 21 mentions that Jesus loved him. I'm sure Jesus didn't stop loving him after he walked away. In fact, I imagine the Lord looked at him with pity. Unfortunately, that young man didn't know what he was walking away from. If people choose to walk away from you, they don't know what they're missing. So don't hate them. Let them walk.

Jesus didn't try to stop him. He didn't try to make him stay. He didn't chase him down. He let him leave. We must let some people leave and love them from a distance. Love never forces itself upon anyone. That young man wasn't willing to go all in for Jesus even though Jesus was willing to go all in for him. Love must be mutual in order for it to be love. If someone is not willing to remain in your love by loving you back, let that person go, and love him or her from a distance.

~Feeling Rejected?~

Ecclesiastes 3:5 teaches us that it is a time to embrace and a time to refrain from embracing. If someone rejects your love, it might be time to refrain from trying to embrace them and begin praying instead. It's all right to express how you're feeling, but after you do, I suggest you let go and allow God.

Don't become bitter. Don't allow your heart to harden. Continue in love. Pray for their heart and pray for God to strengthen you. Pray for His will to be done and rejoice in Him. He'll order the relationship.

~Loving Yourself~

In order for you to love others as yourself, you must love yourself with the eight attributes of love listed in 1 Corinthians 13:4-8. Give yourself the best gift of love by trusting God with your life. Always draw near to Him for mercy in your struggles and time of need. He wants you to do that, so don't ever withdraw from Him.

Be good to yourself. Take care of your physical, emotional, and spiritual health. Remember, the only perfect love is God; therefore, give yourself and others time to grow in His love. Don't try to force anyone to love you. Love must come from a willing heart in order for it to be true love. You can always love from a distance if you need to.

Don't bring harm upon yourself. Don't grieve the Holy Spirit within you by living in sin. Grieving the Spirit zaps your joy. Be kind to yourself. Be patient with yourself. Forgive yourself as God has forgiven you. Refuse to have bitter feelings toward anyone. Bitterness kills your joy. Forgive them. Clear your heart of pain. Jesus will take it all away if you just ask. Do your part by letting go of the past. Live in today while you prepare for your future success.

Don't give up on your dreams. Instead, trust that God will work through you to accomplish them. Living in fear and worry is unhealthy for your mind, body, and spirit. Live in faith instead. Express your needs to God. Always hope for your success and be happy when other people succeed. Be content while striving for a better life. Always tell God how grateful you are for what He has done, what He's doing now, and what He will do in the future. It's good for your health.

~Covenant Responsibility Reminders~

Our Lord Jesus reminds us of our covenant responsibility in John 15:12: "My command is this: Love each other as I have loved you."

John reminds us of our covenant responsibility in 1 John 3:23: "And this is his command: to believe in the name of his Son, Jesus Christ, and to love one another as he commanded us."

The Apostle Paul reminds us of our covenant responsibility in Romans 13:8: "Let no debt remain outstanding, except the continuing debt to love one another, for whoever loves others has fulfilled the law."

James reminds us of our covenant responsibility in James 2:8: "If you really keep the royal law found in Scripture, 'Love your neighbor as yourself,' you are doing right."

~Key Takeaways~

- Your Creator absolutely loves you. Nothing will ever separate you from His love.
- God is the only One who loves perfectly. He sets that example for us to follow.
- God is our Source of love. We draw love from Him so that we have love to give.
- Keeping God's commands to love others is how we prove our love to Him.
- We love Him and others out of a heart that has been cleansed and purified by the blood of Jesus.
- Christ increases love in us as we love Him and others as ourselves.
- Forever see yourself connected to God's love through Christ.
- Love is the mark of every believer.
- Love is holding yourself and others accountable.
- It's ok to love from a distance if you need to.
- Love yourself.
- Unfailing love helps us cultivate strong, meaningful, and lasting relationships.

Chapter 9

That's Not Love

Love…does not envy, it does not boast, it is not proud. It does not dishonor others, it is not self-seeking, it is not easily angered, it keeps no record of wrongs. Love does not delight in evil but rejoices with the truth.
—1 Corinthians 13:4-6

One of the greatest keys to growing in your love for God, others, and yourself, is to know and rid yourself of all the attitudes and behaviors God defines as "unloving" in 1 Corinthians 13:4-6. Along that train of thought, this chapter discusses what love is not and what love does not do.

None of us are exempt from these unloving behaviors and attitudes rising up in our old natures. Becoming more like Christ is a process for all of us. The only immunity we have against these unloving behaviors and attitudes is refusing to live by them. Allowing these unloving ways to rule our hearts, impedes the love of God from flowing freely in us, and from us, onto others. We must cut them out of our hearts with the Sword of the Spirit by living according to God's Word.

True wisdom is applying what we learn. After learning what these unloving behaviors are, working hard not to live by them demonstrates our wisdom.

1. Love Does Not Envy (see 1 Corinthians 13:4)

Be happy when God blesses others. Romans 12:15 says, "Rejoice with those who rejoice...."

A young man received a prestigious award from his job. Everyone shook his hand and congratulated him except the one person he thought would. Surprisingly, that person became very negative toward him and even avoided him for a period of time. As a result, his envy created a sense of disharmony within the workplace.

Envy is nasty. It is unfruitful. We must curse anything that is unfruitful from our lives. Remember, life and death is in the power of the tongue.

Jesus describes envy in Mark 7 as a defilement of the heart, something 1 Peter 2:1 reminds us to get rid of. We do this by choosing to be happy for one another's success, running our own race, and being grateful for what God has blessed us with.

Scripture to reflect on:

James 3:16 says, "For where you have envy and selfish ambition, there you find disorder and every evil practice."

Prayer:

Father, I confess and denounce all forms of envy in my life. I know that all good comes from you. I will not be envious when you choose to bless others. Help me rejoice with those who rejoice. In Jesus' Name I pray, Amen.

2. Love does not boast (see 1 Corinthians 13:4)

Boasting is a form of pride and, therefore, a distraction to God's redemptive work in the world. Boasting takes the glory away from God, who saves souls, and places it on our flesh. If we do boast, let it be in what Christ has done, not only in our lives, but in everyone else's lives, too. If we lift Him up, He will draw souls unto Himself.

Scripture to reflect on:

Galatians 6:14 says, "May I never boast except in the cross of our Lord Jesus Christ, through which the world has been crucified to me, and I to the world."

Prayer:

Father, you alone deserve all the glory. I denounce all forms of boasting from my heart. Help me think about your goodness and forever boast in you. I pray these things in Jesus' Name, Amen.

3. Love is not proud (see 1 Corinthians 13:4)

Pride forms within the heart. Pride is a form of self-centeredness that says, "It's all about me." Pride is thinking we're on a higher plane of existence than everyone else. Pride is thinking we know it all. Pride is unteachable. It is unable to submit to truth. Pride is thinking we're more spiritual than others. Pride is boasting about our abilities, instead of Christ working inside us.

Prideful anger is a relationship killer. It raises the mental walls of hostility, which hinders our relationships from growing in love.

Prideful anger causes us to be consumed with ourselves. It causes us to withdraw from one another instead of drawing near to make peace. When pride is present, no one wants to apologize. We go to sleep angry and wake up with an attitude. Prideful anger hinders us from admitting when we're wrong and saying a humble and sincere, "I'm sorry." Jesus says in Matthew 5:9, "Blessed are the peacemakers, for they will be called children of God."

Pride is an umbrella that God's love beats against. He gives us opportunities to humble ourselves and close the umbrella of pride. That's how we allow His favor to rain down upon us.

Scripture to reflect on:

James 4:6 says, "But he gives us more grace. That is why Scripture says: "God opposes the proud but shows favor to the humble."

Prayer:

Father, I confess and denounce all forms of pride from my heart. I humble myself under the authority of your Word. Help me quickly identify pride forming within my heart and crucify it. In Jesus' Name I pray, Amen.

4. Love does not dishonor people (see 1 Corinthians 13:5)

Love does not dishonor others by words or actions. Words are powerful seeds. With our words, we either sow seeds of life or seeds of death. And since God uses His Word to build us up, it is unloving for us to use our words to tear someone down, especially considering His breath of life is in us. Thus, we should use our words to build each other up. Rude or harsh speech leads to negative interaction. No one wins. You both end up in the negative.

Love does not lessen the value of others. Everyone deserves to be respected. A poor man needs the love of Christ just like a rich man does.

Love does not devalue another person's view. We all want others to respect our viewpoints. A person of love doesn't forget the honor shown to them. They give honor to whom honor is due.

Scripture to reflect on:

Romans 12:10 says, "Be devoted to one another in love. Honor one another above yourselves."

Prayer:

Father, I confess and denounce all forms of dishonorable words, thoughts, and deeds from my life. Help me obey your Word and honor others. In Jesus' Name I pray, Amen.

5. Love is not selfish (see 1 Corinthians 13:5)

I was watching a talk show about troubled relationships. As each couple explained their issues, I notice all of them had the same underlying problem: they were all consumed with their own selfish desires. None of the couples were thinking about serving one another. All I heard was, "I need this" and "I need that." No one asked their mates, "What do you need?"

Jesus reminds us in Matthew 23:11 that the greatest among us is the one who serves. We are not in relationships to only be served; we are in relationships to serve one another. Think about how a relationship would grow if both parties were in it to "out serve" one another.

God is an unselfish God. He gave His Son to die so that we can share in His kingdom. Jesus is an unselfish Lord. He willingly laid down His life for you and me because He valued us above Himself and His desire was the Father's and not His own. Let us, therefore, adopt Christ's spirit of unselfish service to Him and others. Let our desires be the Father's.

Scripture to reflect on:

1 Corinthians 10:24 reads, "No one should seek their own good, but the good of others."

Prayer:

Father, I confess and denounce all of my unselfish ways. I thank you for unselfishly loving me. I desire to love unselfishly and serve others in love. In Jesus' Name I pray, Amen.

6. Love is not quick tempered (see 1 Corinthians 13:5)

God is slow to anger because He's giving the world a chance to accept His love through Christ. If you are in Christ, you will never experience God's day of anger.

Since Jesus was the only perfect person to walk the earth, we must give others an opportunity to repent. God desires all of us to allow for one another's imperfections and faults.

Those who have quick tempers usually make rash decisions, decisions that can destroy their lives and the lives of others. Remember, love is slow to anger.

Scripture to reflect on:

Ecclesiastes 7:9 says, "Do not be quickly provoked in your spirit, for anger resides in the lap of fools."

Prayer:

Father, help me by the power of the Holy Spirit not to become easily angered with others. I denounce having a quick temper. Help me not to take things so personally. I allow you to vindicate me. In Jesus' Name, Amen.

7. Love does not hold onto faults (see 1 Corinthians 13:5)

1 Corinthians 13:5 teaches us that holding others' faults over their heads is unloving, both to yours and others' mental, physical, and spiritual health. It strengthens your mental wall of separation. In order for God to remove the wall that separated us from Him, He wiped away our record of sins. We must do the same for others.

Those who desire to reconcile their relationship must clear the other person of their wrongs. Declare them not guilty. Since that's what God did for us, it would be prideful and unloving for us not to do it for others. A human heart can hurt when it is wronged. Give that hurt to God and bring healing to yourself by letting go. Holding onto it only hurts you. Job 5:2 says, "Resentment kills a fool, and envy slays the simple." Don't allow resentment to kill you from the inside out.

Be reconciled to yourself. Let go of your faults. When you confess from the heart, God forgives you instantly. He cast our faults into the depths of the sea, and we need to do the same for others. Remember, love keeps no record of wrongs.

Scripture to reflect on:

Ephesians 4:32 says, "Be kind and compassionate to one another, forgiving each other, just as in Christ God forgave you."

Prayer:

Father, I confess, denounce, and purge unforgiveness from my heart. I release all who have wronged me of their guilt, just as you have released me of mine. Please touch the hearts of those I have hurt. Allow them to release me of my faults so they may be healed. In Jesus' Name I pray, Amen.

8. Love Does Not Take Pleasure in Evil (see 1 Corinthians 13:6)

All wrongdoing in the eyes of God is evil, which Jesus describes in Mark 7:21-22: "For it is from within, out of a person's heart, that evil thoughts come—sexual immorality, theft, murder, adultery, greed, malice, deceit, lewdness, envy, slander, arrogance and folly."

We can all agree that murder is evil, but how about deceit? How about greed? How about adultery? How about folly? Even though many of us don't see these things as evil, they are because God said so, and His Word is the Truth. His definition counts. So let our personal views be a lie. We must humble ourselves under God's Word and agree with it.

Remember, God hates sin, but He loves the person. So we must hate the sin in our lives and in the lives of our loved ones, but continue to love them as creations of God.

It is unloving to think that what we do in the dark does not affect others. It does. God called us to be light and salt to the world. In Matthew 5:13, Jesus warns us against losing our flavor and tells us in Matthew 5:16 to let our light shine before others.

In short, we must hate anything that diminishes our light or dilutes our salt and prevents Jesus from using us to draw others. That is sincere love for God, self, and others.

Scripture to reflect on:

Romans 12:9 says, "Love must be sincere. Hate what is evil; cling to what is good."

Prayer:

Father, I confess and denounce any love I have for sin. I remove these things far from my heart. I tear down any images I have created within my mind that get in the way of me beholding Your Beauty. Create in me a heart to hate what is wrong and to love what is good according to your Word. In Jesus' Name I pray, Amen.

~Curse Everything Unfruitful~

In Mark 11:14, Jesus curses an unfruitful fig tree: "May no one ever eat fruit from you again." The next day, Peter brought it to Jesus' attention that the tree He cursed had withered from its roots.

Although it was not the season for full-blown figs, the tree should have been producing Taqsh, which is a crop of small knobs, but it wasn't producing any.

We must curse all unfruitful things in our lives. If an action or attitude doesn't produce any nourishment for us, we must denounce it at once. Don't wait around. Do it now. There's power in your spoken word.

Jesus teaches us in verses 22 and 23 that if we believe and do not doubt, whatever we say will happen. Then in verse 24 He tells us to pray, **believe that it is already done**, and it shall come to pass.

Curse unfruitfulness in your life and in your relationships. Declare it dead and pray for fruit that will nourish and strengthen. Believe it is already done, regardless of how it may look now, and the Lord declares it shall happen.

Chapter 10

The 21-Day Love Challenge

"From him the whole body, joined and held together by every supporting ligament, grows and builds itself up in love, as each part does its work."
—Ephesians 4:16

In order to increase love within relationships and connect hearts, each person must do his or her part to build the relationship on God's solid foundation of love. For this reason, I want you and a loved one, whether it be your spouse, fiancé, child, parent, sibling, relative, girlfriend, boyfriend, or best friend to complete the 21-Day Love Challenge together.

You can also complete the Love Challenge as a family or with a fellow believer who has the same desire to grow in God's love as you do. You can even do it by yourself.

The 21-Day Love Challenge is designed to strengthen you and your loved ones in God's love through positive Biblical affirmations of His love, which the Bible teaches strengthen, grows, and sustain us. We transcend to greater love by allowing God to renew our minds concerning how we *view love*. In order to *do love* God's way, we must *view love* His way.

This challenge allows you and your partner to pray together and open the door of communication and consideration for one another on a deeper level. This love challenge also helps you foster an environment of forgiveness, so that you release the past and move toward a healthier and brighter future.

I chose 21 days in order to get everyone into the habit of thinking and talking about how we can better exhibit the attributes of Biblical love toward others and ourselves. You can do it for more than 21 days if you like, however. After all, it's your love challenge. God desires for us to grow in our love for Him and others, and this love challenge is a tool to help us do just that.

The 21-Day Love Challenge consists of the following components:

- ✓ The Love Pledge,
- ✓ The Love Prayer,
- ✓ The Love Affirmation,
- ✓ The Love Assessment, and
- ✓ The Love Calendar.

You can either find all of these documents in the back of the book or download them from The Love Challenge's website at *www.thelovechallenge.us*

Here is a brief description of the documents:

The Love Pledge

The Love Pledge allows you and your partner to pledge to allow the Holy Spirit to help you exhibit Christ's loving attributes toward one another, others, and yourself.

The Love Prayer

The Love Prayer allows you and your partner to invite God into the midst of your session. Matthew 18:20 says, "For where two or three gather in my name, there am I with them."

The Love Affirmation

The Love Affirmation allows you and your partner to declare the love of God over yourselves and the environment of your home. These positive affirmations are Biblical truths that will transform your lives by helping you think, feel, and be vessels of God's love.

The Love Assessment

The Love Assessment allows you and your partner to work on your communication skills. During your weekly check-ins, each person will have the opportunity to express his or her love-needs to one another in a calm and positive manner. The assessment also allows you to examine how well you are exhibiting the eight attributes of Biblical love toward one another and others, and discuss areas of improvement.

The Love Calendar

The Love Calendar is available for you and your partner to set your dates for the initial check-in and follow-ups.

The 21-Day Love Challenge Instructions

Day 1 - Initial Check-In

Love Steps
1. Read, complete, sign, and date "The Love Pledge."
2. Write your meeting dates and times on "The Love Calendar." Assign the Love Guides.
3. Open with "The Love Prayer."
4. Read "The Love Affirmation" aloud. Alternate reading paragraphs or read it together.
5. Conduct "The Love Assessment" discussion.
6. Your love partner will conclude with a positive prayer.
7. Confirm the next meeting date.
8. Set a date night. Do something enjoyable together.

Week 1 - First Check-In

Love Steps
1. Open with "The Love Prayer."
2. Read "The Love Affirmation" aloud. Alternate reading paragraphs or read it together.
3. Conduct "The Love Assessment" discussion.
4. Your love partner concludes with a positive prayer.
5. Confirm the next meeting date.
6. Set a date night. Do something enjoyable together.

Week 2 - Second Check-In

Same as Week 1.

Week 3 - Third and Final Check-In

Love Steps
1. Open with "The Love Prayer."
2. Read "The Love Affirmation" aloud. Alternate reading paragraphs or read it together.
3. Conduct "The Love Assessment" discussion.
4. At the very end of the assessment, discuss your overall growth in each area.
5. Your love partner concludes with a positive prayer.
6. Set a date night. Do something enjoyable together.
7. Continue growing in your love for God, one another, others, and yourself.

These instructions can be downloaded from The Love Challenge's website at ***www.thelovechallenge.us***

Appendix I   *The 21-Day Love Challenge*

The Love Pledge

Ephesians 5:1-2 reminds us to, "Follow God's example, therefore, as dearly loved children and walk in the way of love, just as Christ loved us and gave himself up for us as a fragrant offering and sacrifice to God."

Over the next 21 days, _____ and _____ pledge to allow the Holy Spirit to help us exhibit the following eight attributes of Biblical love toward one another, others, and ourselves:

1. **Patience:** We pledge to follow God's example by being patient with one another, others, and ourselves.

2. **Kindness:** We pledge to follow God's example by being kind to each other, others, as well as ourselves.

3. **Forgiveness:** We pledge to follow God's example and forgive one another, others, as well as ourselves.

4. **Protecting:** We pledge to follow God's example by protecting one another, and ourselves.

5. **Trusting:** We pledge to follow God's example by proving trustworthy with Him, one another, and others.

6. **Hopefulness:** We pledge to follow God's example by hoping for the success of one another, others, as well as ourselves.

7. **Perseverance:** We pledge to follow God's example by persevering with one another, others, and ourselves during adversity.

8. **Unfailing Love:** We pledge to follow God's example by not allowing our love for each other, others, as well as ourselves to grow cold.

Sign:_____ Sign:_____

Date:_____ Date:_____

Appendix II *The 21-Day Love Challenge*

The Love Prayer

Father, we come before Your Throne of Grace and Mercy in Jesus' Name, thanking You for Your Love;

We earnestly desire to strengthen our relationship with You and one another through the bond of love;

We thank You for forgiving and releasing our faults; Today, we forgive and release one another of any past faults;

We release a spirit of unity, peace, and joy within our relationship;

We invite the Holy Spirit to help us to continue to love one another as You have loved us;

We believe all of these things are done in Jesus' Name, Amen.

The Love Affirmation

God loves me. I am forever connected to His love through Christ. I am loving because I draw love from Him. I am loving others as myself; therefore, I am loving to myself.

God is patient with me; therefore, I am patient with others, as well as myself. God is kind toward me; therefore, I am kind toward others, as well as myself. God is unselfish toward me; therefore, I am unselfish toward others.

God is not easily upset with me; therefore, I am not easily upset with others, nor myself. God is not pleased with wrongdoing; therefore, I am not pleased with wronging others, nor myself. God takes pleasure in truth; therefore, I am truthful in my dealings with others, as well as myself.

God forgives and releases my faults; therefore, I am forgiving and releasing the faults of others, as well as my own. God always protects me; therefore, I am always protecting my loved ones, as well as myself. God is trustworthy; therefore, I am proving trustworthy to Him and others.

God always hopes for me; therefore, I am always hoping for the salvation and success of others, as well as my own. God perseveres with me; therefore, I am persevering with others, as well as myself.

God's love for me never fails; therefore, I am forever loving toward others, as well as myself. Each day, I am embracing, enjoying, and expressing the love of God through Christ.

Appendix IV — *The 21-Day Love Challenge*

The Love Assessment

2 Corinthians 13:5 reminds us to examine and test ourselves to see if we're in the faith. Galatians 5:6 reminds us that faith expresses itself in love.

Instructions: Discuss how you walked in love this week by displaying the attributes of Biblical love toward one another, others, and yourself. Take turns as you discuss each point. Be open, honest, humble, and positive.

The Love Assessment	
Patience	Discuss situations where you displayed **patience** with others, one another, and yourself. Discuss situations (lingering or new) where you desire the other person to be more patient with you.
Kindness	Discuss situations where God allowed you to display acts of **kindness** (however slight) toward others? Were you kind to yourself? How? Discuss ways you desire the other person to be more kind to you.
Forgiveness	Discuss whether you had to forgive someone or yourself this week. Is there someone you need to forgive now? Ask the other person to **forgive** you if necessary.
Protecting	How did you protect the Name of God? How did you protect others and yourself? Discuss ways you want the other person to **protect** you and your relationship.
Trusting	Discuss how you displayed **trust** and confidence in God this week. Discuss ways you want the other person to trust you more. How can you improve your trustworthiness with God and others?
Hopefulness	Discuss how hopeful you were with God, others, and yourself. What do you want the other person to **hope** for you?
Perseverance	Discuss situations where you endured in love with others and yourself. Discuss ways you desire the other person to **persevere** with you.
Unfailing Love	Did you reflect on God's **unfailing love** this week? How did you display love toward others and yourself? Discuss ways you want the other person to love you.
Embracing Truth	Did you embrace the truth of God's Word? Did you embrace truth about yourself? Did you speak to someone out of loving truth?
Unloving Behaviors And Attitudes	Discuss your battle with being prideful, envious, boastful, selfish, rude, or quick-tempered. Did you notice any of these creeping into your heart? Did you resist them? Which of these do you need to improve?

*Don't forget to conclude with a thankful and positive prayer!

The Love Calendar

Instructions:

- ✓ Meet with your partner and agree on the start date, check-in dates, and times. Write them below. Check-ins are weekly. Reschedule as needed but be committed.
- ✓ Write down the name of the Love Guide on the calendar. Switch it up each week. The Love Guide is responsible for leading the weekly check-ins.

Tips:

Post your meeting dates and times on your personal calendars.

The Love Calendar			
Event	Date/Time	Name of the Love Guide	Special Instructions
Initial Check-In	_____/_____	_____	Sign and date "The Love Pledge." Follow the love steps.
1st Check-In	_____/_____	_____	Follow the love steps.
2nd Check-In	_____/_____	_____	Follow the love steps.
Final Check-In	_____/_____	_____	Follow the love steps. Discuss overall growth.

⁴ Love is patient, love is kind. It does not envy, it does not boast, it is not proud. ⁵ It does not dishonor others, it is not self-seeking, it is not easily angered, it keeps no record of wrongs. ⁶ Love does not delight in evil but rejoices with the truth. ⁷ It always protects, always trusts, always hopes, always perseveres.

⁸ Love never fails. But where there are prophecies, they will cease; where there are tongues, they will be stilled; where there is knowledge, it will pass away.

1 Corinthians 13:4-8

Relationship With God

A relationship with God is the most important relationship you can have.

Romans 10:9 says, "If you declare with your mouth, "Jesus is Lord," and believe in your heart that God raised him from the dead, you will be saved."

If you want to rededicate or dedicate your life to Jesus, and make Him your Lord and Savior, say this salvation prayer:

Lord Jesus, I confess my sins before you. I believe with all of my heart that You died to take away my sins and You rose again to give me a new life. I confess You as my Lord and Savior. Thank You for washing me clean and giving me everlasting life. Amen.

I Would Like to Hear From You

If you have prayed the salvation prayer or if this book has been a blessing to you, I would love to personally hear from you. Send your testimonies to: **tlc@thelovechallenge.us**

www.ingramcontent.com/pod-product-compliance
Lightning Source LLC
Chambersburg PA
CBHW032123090426
42743CB00007B/447